Parenting
Help from Down in the Trenches

Benny Hunton

ISBN 978-1-0980-6501-0 (paperback)
ISBN 978-1-0980-6502-7 (digital)

Christian Faith Publishing, Inc.
832 Park Avenue
Meadville, PA 16335
www.christianfaithpublishing.com

Printed in the United States of America

My Parenting Story

I have read many books in which the writers would take several pages to thank all the different people who contributed to their work. In most cases, it would be some of the following: family members; work associates; other authors who were involved in the same type pursuits; editors; readers; and many, many others. I too want to take the time here to give a shout-out to so many who, had it not been for them, this book would never have been written. Those you will find here are people that you will never find in most literary publications. I say this not because I do not dearly love them all or because any of them intentionally meant me harm. I very firmly believe that every individual who walks this earth is a human being made in the image of God. We are all unique, and our cultures and upbringings are unique. This is what makes us what and who we are. I also believe that God put in every human that appears on the scenes of this earth a craving for spiritual destiny. I am not saying that all answer those cravings or respond to the calls of a loving God. And this is where my parenting story begins because I thank the Lord daily that I was able to see who he brought into my life right from the very beginning and that through His grace and mercy (which he bestows on every single one of us), I have come to know Jesus.

My parenting story began in Atlanta, Georgia, on October 19, 1942. I was born to a very beautiful young girl and a very handsome young man who evidently placed more importance on the thrills of youth than on the importance of bringing children into a safe and spiritually sound family surrounding. I guess I was more intent on making it in this world than my older siblings because they both died in childbirth. From what I have been told, I also had a difficult time right out of the womb, but I was determined to make it, and I did. I never remember seeing both my father and my mother together; they divorced very soon after I was born. From what I have been told, my father returned from WWII to find that my mother no longer wanted to be married. I think it was a mutual decision. Okay, so not such a good start! My next memories are of a small-framed house on a back street in northwest Atlanta. This was my grandmother's house, and it became *my* house too. And not only my house, but also my cousin's house. His mother (my mother's sister) lived there also. It has been said that a child from the ages of zero to six is forming many traits and habits that will be with them for life. One thing I do know is that I have a "boatload" of memories from that time of my life. I remember standing out at the road and looking down the hill, waiting to see my daddy's old car coming up the hill for a visit. I remember my aunt (not my mother or father) teaching me to ride a bike. I remember almost burning down the old shack next to Mama's (my grandmother) house. I remember making mud pies out in the yard after a rain. I remember asking Mama for a nickel so we could buy a "hunky" from the hunky man who rode by in the summers on his "icebox bike," and I remember her vividly say, "I don't have one red cent." I remember Pawpaw sitting on the front porch, "whittling." I remember one time, he whittled me a rubber-band gun. I remember taking baths in a big aluminum tub right in the living room. One of my favorite memories is of my pawpaw sitting close to his radio receiver, listening to "The Lone Ranger." I could just visualize that white horse rearing up and those silver bullets (I even sent off for one from the back of a cereal box). I could go on and on with memories of this time in my life, but I want to tell you about the best memory I have from Mama's house. On Sunday mornings, we would get ready (my cousin and I), and Mama would walk us to church. After going back to see the old house in the recent past, I would say that the distance from Mama's house to the church was at least half a mile. I remember it like it was yesterday. There were two houses of worship that I remember, and they were across the road from each other. One was at the top of a steep hill, and it was a small, white building with a steeple on top. The other was very unique; it was an old "retired" streetcar (for those of you who might remember streetcars in Atlanta) that sat on its tracks just off the road. We would walk inside and take our seats just like we were getting ready to go to town. The preacher would stand up front and preach away. Mama was my "Lois and Eunice" that Paul talked about to Timothy. One last memory I will mention is that how every single night before we would go to sleep, Mama would come in, and we would do the prayer, "Now I lay me down to sleep. I pray the Lord my soul to keep." I remember trying to take forever in closing those prayers with all the "God bless Mama, God bless Pawpaw, God bless Cousin Norman, God bless Daddy, God bless Mommy" and on and on and on. Certainly, as I look back on those six years, I know without a doubt that my "mama" was God's mercy and grace to me. The turbulent years to come pulled me and swayed me, but it was the memory of that strong, persistent, and truly loving mother figure in my life that held me together.

The parenting picture took on a different look for the next four years. Both my father and my mother found spouses. My father got his life much more together as he and my stepmother started their life together. My mother married an air force pilot, and her troubles continued. I moved to my father's house. He and my stepmother had two other boys, so I became what I deemed in my mind to be the "outsider" in the family. They did nothing to make me feel that way; I did that all by myself. This became a parenting dilemma for the whole family. I spent the third, fourth, and fifth grades in this setting. I am not sure what was going on in all their deliberations, but a decision was made for me to go and live with my mother. She had inherited two daughters in her second marriage. For the next four years, we were all over the place. To begin with, it was one air force base to another; and then after my stepdad received a dishonorable discharge when we were stationed in Hawaii, we returned to California where we lived until I was a sophomore in high school. My mother was not a drinker, but her new husband was. He was not only a drinker but also an alcoholic, and he physically abused my mother regularly. He also physically abused me as well as his two daughters. At one point, all three of us decided to run away due to physical abuse. Needless to say, we did not get very far. We were picked up on a busy Oakland, California, street corner and taken to the police station. The only good thing about this whole incident was that we did not get beaten up that day. My mother finally left this alcoholic abuser, and my life took another twist. I now became a middle schooler with a lot of freedom. It was my mom and me, and she was working most of the time. Things must have gotten too hard for her because the next thing I knew, I was flown back to Atlanta, Georgia. After about a week or two back at dad's, we had a blowup, and the next thing I knew, I was flown back to California. During this time, my mom had met and married her third husband, my second stepdad. He too had children, although much older. All I will say about this is that they were a very bad influence on me. My second stepdad was

7

also an alcoholic. He was an abuser too but more of an emotional abuser. There are so many things that I could go into about his life and lifestyle, but that would not be appropriate here. Eventually, things turned so bad for me in this environment that my mother sent me back to Georgia. I entered school in Atlanta as a tenth grader and graduated in 1960. My school life and church life were very stable. I became a Christian during my junior year. I participated in sports and had lots of friends. I had a good part-time job and was able to purchase my own car during my senior year. I was an active member of our youth group at church and developed close relationships with youth workers and ministers. I had a good friend I met at school who became a Christian. We both decided to go off to college together.

This is as far as I am going to take this parenting story. As you can see, I was not a member of the "ideal family" club. I do want to say that through all the confusion that I have just described, I loved my mother and my father deeply. They both made mistakes, some very critical as far as parenting goes, but they both loved me very much and, in their own ways, tried to provide for me the best they could amid their lives falling apart. I know my stepmother loved me; I don't think I can say that of my stepfathers. It is the unfailing love of my grandmother and the knowledge that I had the love of my mother and my father that took me to college-age and the rest of my life.

In my search for families for the research done in this study, I would never have chosen any of the families in which I grew up with. I would not have given me a chance! I can only thank God of heaven that he raised the right people at the right time who helped guide me through. I could mention many whom I encountered in my Christian college experience who were there for me at just the right time. I hope you can see in all this why I have devoted my whole life to working with young people from all kinds of backgrounds, hoping and praying all along that none of them would have to experience many of the things I went through. The greatest tool, first of all, is to have someone in their lives who genuinely cares and that hopefully, they will have both a mother and a father to guide their home and also that these parents will practice biblical principles of parenting. You will see throughout this work the admonition, *"Make sure the message of love gets through!"* As Peter said, "Love covers a multitude of sins." This principle is so true in the parenting realm. If Mom and Dad get the message of love across clearly, they will have a lot of room to mess up.

Introduction

What you are about to experience in the following pages is a glimpse into the family lives of some very faithful, God-fearing, and loving parents. You will be that "fly on the wall" in their day-to-day grind of family living. None of the mothers and fathers or their children ever authored a parenting book. None held workshops or taught seminars on raising successful children. None hold degrees in family counseling or child psychology; however, most do hold college degrees. Every one of these participating sets of parents in this study is a middle-income, hard-working, tax-paying, law-abiding citizen. So what I am trying to say is that the parents in this research are a lot like so many of us. You will see as I have that they were able to have success in the most important task given to a man and a woman: "Do not exasperate your children; instead, bring them up in the training and instruction of the Lord" (Eph. 6:4). Jesus used a little child as an analogy to a believer and made the following statement, "If anyone causes one of these little ones, those who believe in me, to stumble, it would be better for them to have a large millstone hung around their neck and be drowned at the bottom of the sea" (Matt. 18:6). There is no doubt that children, by their very nature, are a high priority to our Creator. The couples in this research totally espouse this concept. The results they achieved speak for themselves.

It may be of interest to you to know the motivating factors behind this research. This work comes as a result of a lifetime of working with children of all ages, both my own children and others' children. I have been blessed to work in the education field (elementary, middle school, and high school). I have also had opportunities to interrelate with the youth through athletics and youth ministry. Time and space would not allow me to share here the thousands of interactions I have been blessed to experience with the youth of all ages. I could safely say that most of those interactions have been positive, and some were not so positive. Many of those young folks were so teachable, almost like a sponge, and some were extremely difficult to teach. Most were cooperative, and some balk in every step of the way.

During all this, I began to wonder, What causes one child to be so cooperative while another is basically disobedient? What causes one child to possess such a great attitude while another is so resentful and bitter? How can one player be so coachable while another has to be prodded every step of the way? Why are some kids so confident and ready to learn while others lack self-motivation or a desire to learn? Granted, there are many directions to go for complete answers to these and many other questions; however, there is one common denominator in the lives of every child. That common ground is that every child, be it an elementary, middle school, or high school student, came out of an environment called home. Yes, there are many variables but one constant. Is this not the very attribute that is the object of research—to find the "constant" and to find the one thing held in common? It is this phenomenon of "home" that drew my attention. This is the one area that stands out among all others that became the object of my efforts to discover the why behind the myriad of childhood outcomes that I was seeing in the classes I taught in schools, in youth activities and classes at church, and in everyday life.

Do you believe that success breeds success? Do you feel that if you surround yourself with successful people, you will be more likely to have a successful endeavor, no matter what that endeavor is? If you find that every time you give a certain person a task, that task is completed efficiently and on time; but every time that same task is given to another individual, there has been a failure that you defer to the first individual. All these are illustrations of the truth that success is usually attained by success-oriented people. I looked around, long and hard, at the young people I have been blessed to teach and coach. Some had success, and some, not so much. My own shortcomings as a teacher and coach naturally fit into the big picture also, and I take ownership of that. However, I also look at the "common thread" woven through this whole experience. I am brought back once again to the root, the origin, and the years of cultural environment called home.

I could have very easily made a trip down to the local bookstore to begin checking out what all the professionals are saying about successful parenting. I might have searched for an appropriate training session or seminar. I might even have turned to preachers and other church leaders to get their input on this very important life principle. The reality is each one of these areas of expertise is a very valid source of parenting help. There are excellent books that have a lot of valuable information and great insights. There are also many great speakers and authorities who have done a lot of research who have helped thousands of seekers of parenting information and tips. Every congregation has leaders and teachers who share timely and valuable truths to help parents deal with their children. Both as a parent and as a professional in the counseling field, I have made numerous purchases of books and materials, traveled hundreds of miles to sit at the feet of presenters in training sessions, and have had many discussions with good and faithful servants in the local congregations. One thing I noticed in the world of books, seminars, and close brothers and sisters of faith is that the one greatest source for information about parenting is strikingly absent: *the parents themselves!* I began searching for such a book or parent-led seminar. You may know of such of book. You may be aware of this kind of research. But I did not locate any. As a result of this line of thinking, a "vision" was born. How great it would be to go "down into the trenches" of parenting as it happened and as it is happening and gain those types of insights.

Having never actually done this type of research, I pondered so many different aspects of such a project: How would I get willing participants in this research? What kind of questioning would I use? How would I determine who would be the subjects of the research? What were the possible variables in this research? How much time would be involved? What would be the cost of such an undertaking? All these and many more questions came into consideration. To be truthful, my vision of pulling together pertinent and helpful information for parents became an overwhelming and daunting process of thought. And then as is often the case, passion trumped human reality! This kind of information and insight is not only important but necessary. This can happen; this will happen.

My first task was to find willing participants and not only willing but also appropriate ones. There are many quips, quotes, and analogies that come to mind here (i.e., "You know a tree by the fruit it bears" and "The proof is in the pudding" being just a couple). I had in mind so many young people and their parents who were such a joy to work with. I wanted to take this research just a little further. Not only was I concerned with what I was blessed to experience by having these wonderful young people in my classes and on the teams that I coached, but also I was focusing on long-term benefits of loving and quality parents. I wanted to locate parents who were not only successful in bringing their children through all the tough times of elementary, middle school, and high school. I wanted to find out how and what these parents did during those critical years that eventually translated into raising successful individuals, successful marital partners, and successful parents themselves. The couples in this research are comprised of individuals, and couples of various ages and life situations. Some of them are couples who have children still at home. Some are parents who have older children who have left the home and started families of their own. Some are older couples whose children have young-adult children themselves. I have been privileged to be part of their lives to some extent, and some, very deeply. Across the board, though, every one of them was an inspiration to me personally and in my work as a teacher, coach, youth minister, and professional counselor.

My second task was to inform each of the participating couples of the purpose of the research and to acquaint them with what would be expected of them. Each parent (both the mother and the father), filled out a separate inventory of questions regarding their family origins. There were fifty questions in this part of the inventory. Next, both the mother and the father worked together with a second series of questions regarding their present family. There were sixty-five questions in this part of the inventory. There was one more set of questions that the parents answered regarding the present state of their children since college or later. There were twenty questions in this part of the inventory.

Upon receiving the responses from each of the participating couples, I then began the task of pulling together results, calculating percentages relative to the various categories of information, and finally, drawing conclusions. It was the obvious hope that I pursued, which was to glean from these families, parenting principles that worked. I hoped that by going right to the source—"parents down in the trenches"—I would be able to see not from a book or some professional educator techniques that have been proven to be successful. I know they worked because I saw the results; they were visible in the lives of real people.

Gauging Successful Parenting

Some might argue that these two words just do not go together. Some would be quick to argue, "There are no perfect parents!" which would be true. Of course, in the grand scheme of things on this planet, to parent in such a way as to produce Bible-believing, God-fearing, and authentic Christlike living would be the ultimate success. We need not go any farther, end of discussion. However, through this research, I have been made aware of some of the "tangibles" in the process of attaining this goal. This does not require the "perfect parent," and every step will not be labeled a *success!*

With these thoughts in mind, consider the following supposition: *There are particular parenting approaches, processes, techniques, and advisements that will produce the following type of adult.* There is

- a 96%–100% chance they will not only attend a post-secondary educational institution but will achieve their BS, BA, MA, or PhD if they so desire;

- a 90%–100% chance they will live both financially, physically, and emotionally independent of their parents;
- a 92%–100% chance they will marry, have children, and will never have lived in a cohabiting relationship before marriage;
- an 88%–90% chance they would never divorce;
- a 95%–100% chance they will be in church regularly and a 70%–75% chance they will be a teacher in Bible classes where they attend;
- a 100% chance they will never be arrested;
- a 70%–75% chance they will be alcohol-free;
- a 100% chance they will be tobacco-free;
- an 80%–87% chance they will be involved in community improvement efforts in the areas where they live; and
- a 95%–100% chance they will be directly involved in community outreach in the churches they attend.

Sound incredible? Yes! Without a doubt, these parenting outcomes are discussed often in terms of "lofty goals" or sometimes "pie in the sky" hopes, yet I have found them to be present and ongoing in the lives of the offspring of the parents in this study—and not just present but also existing at the high percentage rates listed.

I wanted to know, what did these parents do? How did they manage to produce such amazing results with the children growing up in their homes? What were their secrets? Well, thankfully, these parents have been willing to share their parenting experiences with us. These skills do not come to us in the form of "parenting principles 101" but more like "a way of life." In fact, in answer to one of the questions in the survey, "Did you or your spouse ever take a parenting class?" the answer was pretty much, "No," except for what was taught or discussed at their place of worship. Their parenting approaches were basically a way of life for them, and they worked to engrain this into their children. Their own parents, although living in a drastically different time and culture, passed on a lot of these parenting principles to them. Sounds a lot like what Paul once said in 2 Timothy 1:5 (ERV),

> I remember your true faith. That kind
> of faith first belonged to your grand-
> mother Lois and to your mother Eunice.
> I know you now have that same faith.

I am very excited now to begin sharing with you, the reader, all the wonderful and usable insights of these parents. I hope that if you are not already practicing the principles you see here, you will begin incorporating and applying them as you see fit into your own parenting scenario. The key phrase here is *as you see fit*. Certainly, not all their approaches in parenting their children will be a natural fit in your family. Without a doubt, though, you will find principles that do work. Thank you for taking the time to consider this unique research as one of the most important, if not the most important, tasks given to mankind—raising independent, responsible, productive, and Christian offspring. Jesus himself said, "Let the little children come unto me, for of such is the kingdom of God" (Matt. 19:14).

Statistical Data

The Families That Produced the Parents in Our Study

It may be worthwhile to look first at where these successful parents came from. What were their growing-up years like? How were they parented? The following are the questions in the survey and the answers along with the percentages attached. Some of this information are meaningful, and some, not so much.

- 54% came from rural settings and 46% urban or suburban.
- The average number of siblings in their families was two to three.
- 32% were the oldest children, 25% youngest, and 43% were middle children.
- 68% of their parents were employed outside the home.

- 14% of their parents attained an HS education, 47% attained some college or a college degree, 38% attained a master's degree, and 1% attained a PhD.
- 77% attended public schools, 17% attended private schools, and 6% attended both public and private schools.
- 68% of their parents participated in sports.
- 50% of their parents participated in the arts.
- 80% of their parents never experienced having stepparents.
- 67% of their parents held leadership positions in their respective high schools.
- 93% of their parents never divorced.
- 96% of their parents attended church regularly.
- 86% of their parents were considered by these parents as having a sincere faith.
- 69% of their parents had been members of a youth group at the churches they attended.
- 73% of their parents attested to having a "mentor" while growing up, and 45% of the time it was a teacher or coach, 22% of the time it was a youth minister or minister, and a small percentage named the grandmother as the mentor.
- 50% of their parents were either in the mid- to low-average income.
- 50% of their parents often had company over to their houses; 41% seldom had company over.

- 60% of their parents lived near their grandparents.
- 100% of their parents required chores for their children.
- 68% of their parents did not serve in the military.
- 45% of their parents were "highly" involved in their respective churches, 14% were somewhat involved, 22% with some involvement, and 14% were never involved.
- 86% of their parents were unpaid church staff.
- 57% were church leaders (i.e., elders, song leaders, class teachers, etc.).
- 73% of their parents (either mom or dad) were Bible teachers in their respective churches.
- 50% of their parents attended church summer camps.
- 68% of their parents attended youth rallies.
- 77% of their parents had Christian relatives.
- 73% of their grandparents were Christians.
- 77% of their parents never drank alcohol.
- 64% of their grandparents never drank alcohol.
- 50% of their parents used tobacco to some level.
- 30% of their parent's relatives did not use alcohol, 30% were casual drinkers, and 1% were heavy drinkers.
- 45% of their mothers were the spiritual leaders in their homes, 32% of the spiritual leaders were the dads, and 16% had no spiritual leaders.

- 18% of their parents had devotionals in their homes.
- 64% of their parents went on vacation with the family.
- 100% of their parents practiced corporal punishment in the home.
- The last time these parents could remember receiving a spanking from their parents was between the ages of eleven and fourteen.
- 32% of their parents set limitations on time watching TV.
- 86% of their parents placed restrictions on types of movies to be watched.
- 98% of their parents set a dating age to commence at ages fifteen to sixteen.
- 73% of their parents set dating curfew times— 95% was 11:00 p.m.

Pulling It Together

What Would It Look Like?

The parents of all the remarkable kids in our survey most likely came up in either a rural or suburban setting as their home. The total number in their family probably numbered about five—mother, father, and two or three children on average. Since their income was in the low to middle range, Mom had to take on a job outside the home to help with expenses. The kids attended the local public schools and were active in sports and other activities. They were outgoing for the most part and held leadership positions in their school. Their parents were not divorced, so they did not have to endure the hardships of what that brings into families. Sundays always found them in church. The kids saw in their parents a spiritual genuineness: they practiced what they preached. They were hospitable to their neighbors and their church family; they were found having them over to the house very often. The grandparents lived in proximity, so they got to be with them a lot. The parents had regular chores that they required of the kids. The family value system seemed to be centered around the "church" and church activities. Either Mom or Dad or both were teachers of classes at church, and Dad was among the leaders in the church, serving as an elder, deacon, or song leader. Since the grandparents lived close by, they were at church also. The parents encouraged the kids to be part of youth activities and summer camps. About the only alcohol consumption ever seen was in some of the extended family or relatives. Mom was usually the spiritual leader in the home, but Dad also took this role. A lot of the time, it was joining in together. The family took vacations together during summers. As far as discipline was concerned, when the kids disobeyed, corporal punishment was sure to follow. Time was somewhat limited for TV, and movie-going was monitored very closely. The kids were not allowed to date until around age fifteen or sixteen, and the normal curfew was 11:00 p.m.

Your first response from this synopsis of family life from days gone by might well be, "What planet did these people come from?" or, "It just doesn't happen that way anymore." Yet another response that I imagine might enter into your thinking would be, "What does this have to do with me? My family of origin is nothing like this. In fact, mine was just the opposite. If this is what it takes to become a successful parent, then I am hopeless, and not only me but my children as well." I totally understand such logic. I too grew up in home situations that were vastly different from the one I have described here. I had to struggle, I made many mistakes, and I had not been a model parent. I have three wonderful children. They have wonderful children, and I will continue to be there for them as Dad as long as they call on me. I continue to see progress in each one of my children, especially spiritually. The Lord constantly blesses me with opportunities to instill better parenting skills and techniques in the lives of my children (even though they do not live with me anymore) as well as in the lives of others around me.

I realize too that times have changed. We live in a time when the culture and customs of these days are drastically different from past generations. Our struggles are different from times past. As your children walk out your door in the morning and head off to day care or school, the things they have to deal with are much different from what you or your parents had to deal with as children.

Herein lies the importance of this research because this research is one that is based on principles rather than how-tos. There are concepts and principles that we can see through this research that are valid, no matter what the era or time frame, that resulted in success both for parent and child. In this study, there are three generations of note, involving 85 to 105 years of parenting experiences ranging from the mid-1930s to the early 2020s. There is also an emerging generation of children on the way as infants and toddlers that will take these parenting effects well into 2040 and beyond. In the area of athletics, there is a term that is thrown around called dynasty. It is used to refer to a team that has such a good recruiting and coaching system that it enjoys success in wins over several seasons or years. How much greater it would be to have generations of successful parents who have been able to engrain into their offspring principles of righteous living and spirituality that they, in turn, engrain into their offspring—a dynasty of family, childhood, and parenting success that endures through many generations.

Statistical Data

The Parents in Our Study

We now turn our attention to the families that produced the amazing results we see in this study. Take note of the achievements:

- About 3/4 (72%) of these families lived in suburban settings; the rest lived in rural settings.
- Most averaged three children in the family.
- About 3/4 (72%) were families in which both parents worked outside the home.
- All these families were highly educated. 100% of the fathers had a bachelor's degree or higher, and 64% of the mothers had a bachelor's degree or higher.
- 97% of these children were involved in athletics in their respective schools; 64% were involved in the Arts.
- 64% of the children attended private schools.

- 91% of these children never experienced divorce in their families.
- 100% of these children were regular in church attendance, and 90%–95% were members of their respective church's youth group activities.
- These families were mostly middle-income levels financially (82%).
- The parents and children were very likely to have friends and/or neighbors over regularly (72%).
- There was only about a 45% chance of the grandparents living nearby; more than half were deceased or lived far away.
- 100% of the children in this research had chores expected of them.
- 100% of the parents in this study were considered "highly active" in their respective churches.
- 45% of the parents in this study were some level of a paid religious worker.
- 100% of the parents were in church leadership positions or teachers.
- 73% of these children had attended church camps; 91% had attended youth rallies with their respective youth groups.
- 91% of their relatives in their extended families were Christians.
- None of these children had consumed alcohol at any time in these families.
- 91% had never experienced any tobacco usage.

- Over half of these kids had no extended family that used tobacco or alcohol.
- The father was the spiritual leader in 100% of these families.
- 82% of these families took regular vacations.
- Corporal punishment was administered in 91% of these families.
- The amount of time watching TV was not a huge issue, and 91% of these families allowed movie-going (but with restrictions as to the type of movie [100%]).
- The average dating age was fifteen to sixteen, and curfew times were observed.
- In 70% of the families, discipline was handled by both parents.
- Rewards for good behavior was practiced in only 30% of these parents.
- 60% of the parents gave allowances, and half of these were with stipulations as to how it was to be used or spent.
- Only 35% of these children had ever worked in a garden, but 91% helped in meal preparation. Only 91% customarily did yard work around the house.
- 91% of these children had a part-time job at some point; 73% had a checking and savings account.
- 73% of the children felt their parents were totally unified in their parenting efforts while

the other 27% felt their parents were mostly unified.

- 100% of the children visibly saw their parents being affectionate toward one another in the home, 73% saw very little argument, and 27% witnessed some strife.
- 75% of the families had no taboo areas of discussion; all topics were on the table.
- The parents said that in 100% of the cases, their children felt equally loved.
- The parents said that in 100% of the cases, spirituality was the number one family value.
- The parents said that in 100% of the cases, quality family time was a chief goal while at the same time, they felt that their careers got in the way (about 50% of the time).
- 100% of children were allowed to have differing opinions from the parents
- 100%, failure was okay.
- 100%, children had attended funerals.
- 75% of parents were considered strict.
- 65% of parents were considered firm.

Pulling It All Together

What Would It Look Like?

These families were middle income and suburban. They were families of four or five in number, and they lived in the southern part of the United States. The family, both parents and children, were very active in their communities as well as their churches. The children were also very busy at home due to the chores given to them to keep the home front going. Education was important to the parents, and they expected this of their children. All parents had either been to college or had achieved a college diploma. Every one of the fathers had at least a bachelor's degree and one a PhD. Practically every male and most females had participated in their school's athletic programs. Most had engaged in the arts, whether it be the performing type or in fine arts (i.e., painting, drawing, sculpture, etc.). Most children in this research attended private schools or small public schools. Many went on to attend Christian universities after graduation. None of the children in this research ever experienced divorce firsthand (their parents). Every one of these children was regular in church attendance, and not only regular but also were active members of their youth groups. They were also interactive with other youth groups through their attendance at youth rallies and summer Bible camps regularly. The parents had friends, neighbors, and church families over often. In a lot of cases, the grandparents did not live very close by; and in some cases, some were already deceased. Spiritual leadership was an extremely high-priority item, both in the home and the local church. Most parents held some type of leadership position in the church—some Bible class teachers, some song leaders, some elders, and some deacons. The children not only had their parents as spiritual leadership examples, but their extended family members also held the same Christian values. It is of value to note that not one child in this research ever saw alcohol being consumed at home. It is also of special note that most of these children never saw a cigarette being lit there. In the home, there was a father and a mother who cooperated in spiritual leadership with the father taking the lead.

The following are a few more items that came out in the research that may or may not be considered as critical to successful parenting:

- Most of these families took family vacations.
- In the area of discipline, corporal punishment was the "tool of choice." This is not saying that spanking/physical pain was used but that

children lived in a consequential environment. Discipline was dually administered. Rewards and/or bribes were not used as incentives for good behavior.

- Only about half of the parents gave allowances to the children, and about that same number had checking or savings accounts. Practically, every child in this research had a part-time job at some point in high school.

- The parents stressed being on the same page—in other words, unity in their approach to the children—and they felt the children saw and understood this unity in their leadership of the family.

- It was important that the children actually "beheld" their parent's affection for one another. Hugging, kissing, and holding hands were common sights in these homes.

- Movie-going was allowed in these families but with strong restrictions as to the type of movie watched.

- Quality time for the family to be together was extremely important. These parents lamented the fact that their jobs and careers got in the way of this many times.

- These families were "open communication" families. There were no taboo topics; all things were invited to be on the table for discussion.

- Failure was not necessarily a negative trait in these families but rather something that often led to success or a lesson learned.
- Overall, the children saw their parenting experience as loving and firm or loving and strict.

There is a very popular tool that is being used around the world these days that enables individuals to research their ancestral backgrounds to discover information about "roots" or family beginnings. I as well as possibly hundreds of thousands of others (maybe millions) have discovered things they never knew about their personal origin and special family traits. Many have been able to come to a better understanding of themselves in the *now* and bring the pieces together regarding their heritage and who they are. In this research, I have been able to focus on three specific generations of different families. This goes back to the earlier 1900s and proceeds as far in the future as 2040 or beyond. I saw happy, productive offspring who were accomplishing and practicing all the things that most of us could only hope that our kids will achieve in this world. I saw it over and over in these families and began to put two and two together and began asking questions to find out their secrets. I always wanted my children to achieve special things in this life, and here is a description of what I was seeing around me in these families that I was allowed to experience firsthand:

- I wanted my children to get an education. These kids were achieving this at a 95%–100% success rate.

- I wanted my children to learn how to be self-supporting and independent. These kids were accomplishing this at a 90%–100% success rate.
- I wanted my children to meet and marry and grow their own families with someone they loved and who loved them *and* would never cohabit with anyone before marriage. These kids were practicing this at a 92%–100% success rate.
- I did not want my children to ever experience a divorce. These kids were accomplishing this at an 88%–90% success rate.
- I wanted my children to become Christians, be faithful in their attendance, and even become class teachers and leaders. These kids were 95%–100% in attendance every Sunday and 70%–75% likely to be teaching a class there.
- God forbid that any of my children would ever be arrested. 100% of these kids had never been—and hopefully never will—be arrested.
- I would choose for my children to abstain from alcohol. These kids were 70%–75% sure to remain alcohol-free.
- Likewise, I wanted my kids never to pick up the tobacco habit. These kids were 100% tobacco-free and hopefully always will be.
- I would love for my children to be community-minded in the areas where they live. These

kids were 80%–87% involved in their respective communities.

- I saw the importance of every Christian becoming active in taking the Gospel to a lost world. I wanted this for my children. These kids were 95%–100% involved in doing this very thing.

So as the Christmas song says, "Do you see what I see? Do you hear what I hear?"

We now know the grandparents, the parents, and the very kids themselves. We have learned about what it was like to grow up in the early to mid-1900s. We know somewhat about the '50s, '60s, and '70s, and we have looked at the offspring into the '90s and 2000s. There are already young toddlers and children who are beginning to forge their ways through this life and will be the teens and college students of the 2030s and 2040s. I feel very confident about this generation we have been examining. I feel they will follow the course that has been set for them. How fortunate they are to have had such a strong and stable ancestry. The concern I have is for *us*! How will we be able to survive?

Lois and Eunice

I must emphasize again the "Lois and Eunice" principle of parenting. Paul had mentioned these two wonderful examples in his letter to Timothy. Paul attributed to these two women the spiritual strength that was evident in the life of Timothy. It is a powerful thing to behold what God can do through Christ-filled, Spirit-led parenting. It is not a guarantee that children will *always* choose to follow the Lord, but as we have seen in this research, the expectations are high and the probabilities are more sure. I must turn my attention to the scenario in which there is no Lois and Eunice principle at work in the life of a child. This research has helped in bringing some resolution to this dilemma. In more than one of these family scenarios, the Lois and Eunice parenting principle was absent. We sometimes quote the sentiment expressed by Mordecai when he was persuading Esther to speak to the king, "And who knows, maybe you have been chosen to be the queen for such a time as this." God works through his Spirit to use us in ways that we may not even realize or understand.

I remember being in transit from the school where I worked to another school, and one of the parents in this study happened to be with me at the time. I remember him vividly explaining to me as we passed an old, dilapidated barn-looking structure just off the highway yet clearly visible from the road that he used to live in that structure with his sister and his mother. He went on to explain what it was like to live in those conditions. I am not sure how long it was after that when he and his siblings came to live in the children's home that was associated with the school where I worked, but he and his sister were brought into our care. The Lord brought me to this same organization for employment, and I soon had the privilege of becoming a teacher, coach, and mentor to this diamond in the rough. There were others involved with these two children by becoming the "village that raised the child." There was one memorable set of what we termed at the time "house parents" who had a life-changing effect on this child. They took the time to do one main thing: *get the message of love across*! I have heard him express this sentiment about this family many times.

So in the absence of the Lois and Eunice parenting principle, parenting success can still happen. It will involve quality time, genuineness, godly example, and making sure the message of love gets across. It will be even more securely ingrained if this message comes from more than one vantage point; it will take a village!

This is a special note to you, the reader, of my ramblings. I am presuming that you have a genuine interest in the parenting process. I am not aware of what you bring to the table, so to speak. You may have come to this place and time, following the experience of a Lois-and-Eunice atmosphere. On the other hand, you may have a parenting background or culture void of loving, nurturing parenting experience. Please consider this: *there is no better time or place to start than the present!* You can be the generation that your children, grandchildren, and great-grandchildren will view as being the heritage that was responsible for the spiritual strength that they, as parents, now possess. So whether you came up as a child with strong Christian leadership and a clear message of love or as a child void of these parenting elements, you must recognize that you *are* "the next generation." It is your place to give to the generation that succeeds you.

We have all heard the negative cry, "Spiritual apathy is only one generation away." There is another negative sentiment out there, which is, "Spiritual apathy in parents breeds spiritual demise in children." In other words, the general tendency will be that children will experience a *decrease* in faith when their parents do not practice a genuine everyday faith themselves. I am not saying—nor do I believe—that mere church attendance or "pew-packing" (as it is sometimes labeled) is the answer. As I mentioned previously, spending quality time with each child and the family as a whole, genuineness in everyday living, portraying godly examples learned in Scripture and, most importantly, making sure the message of love is routinely getting through are essential ingredients of successful and godly parenting.

A valuable thought in this discussion that brings hope to hurting parents who sometimes feel that they are failures as their children's caregivers is that parents do not have to be adept and especially not perfect in this. We all fall short in many and sometimes *all* these areas. Emphasis needs to be made here that the one overriding principle to make sure of is that *the message of love gets across*! A parent may fall short in many ways. He/she may have personality traits that get in the way constantly. There may be circumstances over which neither parent has the control that must be faced daily, *but every parent can make sure the message of love gets across to each child and the family as a whole.* As Peter wrote, "Above all, love each other deeply, because love covers a multitude of sins" (1 Pet. 4:8).

The Significant Seven

Attention will now be given to the Significant Seven. The families under consideration in this research were presented with sixty-five different components of the parenting experience. Each set of participants responded to questions relative to all sixty-five components. Each couple shared their own experiences in dealing with each of the parenting scenarios relating to these components. They would describe what it was like at their house. For this research, which was to glean from successful parents the techniques they incorporated in their successful parenting experiences, I have narrowed the scope of our attention to what I call the Significant Seven. This research resulted in bringing together a vast number of significant areas of importance to those searching for tools and/or techniques that would help them in parenting their own children. It was of interest to me to know the best of the best. Since seven is a number in Scripture that denotes "completeness" or "fullness," I chose to bring together the top seven areas that these successful parents related to being across the board and unanimously important in the parenting process. I chose only those areas that had a 90%–100% agreement rate with every responding couple. Although there were many areas of very high agreement (often in 80% of the couples), I chose to rather include in the significant seven only those principles that achieved the 95%–100% agreement rate. Every area will be included for you in this book; however, I feel that special emphasis needs to be placed on those items in which 95% of the couples basically said, "These are the seven most important principles of parenting that we practiced in raising our children to be what they are today."

You will notice two lists below. The first is a list of family values. The second is a list of parenting principles. There are seven in each list. These are the seven areas mentioned above—those top seven areas that the parents in this study deemed most important to the parenting process. I have listed them first as a family value and then secondly as a parenting principle. In the first list, the term *family value* is used because the family saw it as important to their family. It was not something they read in a book or learned in a parenting class; it was a principle that they practiced many times because they had been brought up that way in their own families of origin or as a result of simply knowing Jesus and wanting their children to know him also. The second list is the principles of life that correlate with the value— sometimes spiritually based and sometimes logically or commonsense based.

Significant Seven list 1 (family values)

1. Our children had personal and spiritual involvement with other like-minded peers.
2. Our children had role models within their own families who practiced their faith genuinely and authentically.
3. Our children were given responsibilities of work, both within the family (chores) and outside the family (part-time jobs).
4. Our children enjoyed the freedom of expression. They were allowed to have an opinion and the "freedom to fail" and that being okay, all within the umbrella of a consequential environment.
5. Our children were not subjected to an addictions environment (alcohol, drugs, and tobacco). We did not practice the use of these addictive substances and did not allow our children to do such.
6. Our children enjoyed quality time with us, parents. When there were siblings, each child experienced personal quality time with each parent or both.
7. Our children participated in athletics.

We see here seven family values practiced by every one of these successful parenting couples. Of special note is the order in which these values are listed. They are listed in the order of top-down. In other words, the value listed as number one is the top-rated family value. The value rated number seven (athletic participation) is not a low rating; it came in at a 97% practice rate. All seven of these family values were practiced by 95%–100% of the families in this research. You will now see below these family values translated into the form of "principles" that these families deemed important enough to engrain into the lives of their children.

Significant Seven list 2 (parenting principles)

1. Second Corinthians 6:14: "*Do not be unequally yoked with unbelievers. For what partnership has righteousness with lawlessness? Or what fellowship has light with darkness?*" This is the relationship principle of a healthy balance as it pertains to friendships ("Be not yoked together with unbelievers. Surround yourself with successful people.").

2. James 2:18: "*But someone will say, you have faith and I have works. Show me your faith apart from your works, and I will show you my faith by my works.*" This is the parenting principle of *actually living* before the children what is taught in the Word ("Practice what you preach.").

3. Second Thessalonians 3:10: "*For even when we were with you, we would give you this command: if anyone is not willing to work, let him not eat.*" This is the principle of working for what you get ("If a man does not work, let him not eat.").

4. Ephesians 6:4: "*Fathers, do not provoke your children to anger, but bring them up in the discipline and instruction of the Lord.*" This is the parenting and relationship principle of being allowed to exist in an atmosphere of encouragement rather than harshness with no room to fall short and learn from mistakes ("the freedom to be me").

5. Second Timothy 2:22: "*So flee youthful passions and pursue righteousness, faith, love, and peace, along with those who call on the Lord from a pure heart.*" This is the moral principle of abstinence as it relates to the vices of Satan in this world (i.e., alcohol, drugs, and other such things). Also involved here is the principle of unhypocritical living on the part of the parents ("clean living").

6. John 8:9–11: "*And Jesus was left alone with the woman standing before Him. Jesus stood up and said to her, Woman, where are they? Has no one condemned you? She said, No one, Lord. And Jesus said, Neither do I condemn you; go and from now on sin no more.*" This is the relationship principle of giving undivided attention to those you really care for and for those you want to help succeed.

7. First Timothy 4:8: "*For while bodily training is of some value, godliness is of value in every way, as it holds promise for the present life and also for the life to come.*" This is the principle of competitiveness and physical exercise ("lessons from the field of play").

The Application and Practical Application of the Significant Seven

We come now to the second most important part of this whole endeavor: *the application*. This is what motivated my research. Following the application principle, you will then see what I call *the practical application*. As I looked out and saw what appeared to be successful spiritual young people practicing all the things that successful Christian young people do (who are meeting and marrying other successful young people and who are vibrant members of society and the church), I wanted to know what these parents did that produced such wonderful kids. I found out that these parents were not perfect people. They would probably never consider themselves to be ideal parental examples. They would probably be heard saying such things like, "God blessed us with great kids!" "We could not have done this without God in our lives." "Thanks to the village around us!" or "Our parents (their grandparents) showed us the way." This attitude is another reason why these couples are so successful; they appeared to be humble in spirit and open to change.

Application 1

These Successful Parents Were Very Careful Not to Allow Their Children to Become "Unequally Yoked" with Other Young People Who Were Not of the Same Mindset as They Were. Positively Speaking, These Parents Made It a Priority to Ensure That Their Children Experienced Personal Spiritual Involvement with Other Children of the Same Mindset.

Please note here that this principle does *not* imply that these children weren't allowed to associate with other children who didn't share similar spiritual views and commitments as themselves. It *does* say, however, that they were not allowed to become "unequally yoked" with them. There is a huge difference here. Our Savior was found in many settings in which he associated with people of questionable reputation (i.e., the adulterous woman [John 8], the tax collectors [Luke 19], the unethical businessman [Luke 16], and many others). The successful parents in our study noted that they took the parental prerogative to help their children through these questionable friendships at school and in the community. As any parent will testify, this is not always an easy parenting task. Many variables come into play such as the age of the child, the maturity level of the child, the personality of the child, the school and community environment of the child, and much more. It is one thing to develop childhood friendships and to engage in play at school and the neighborhoods, and it is totally different when our children lose sight of family values and what is important in the big spiritual picture to maintain their friendships in the world. The parents in this study were able to help their children maintain balance. I am sure that there were many occasions when things got out of balance. Stephen Glenn, in his book *Raising Self-Reliant Children in a Self-Indulgent World*, made the statement, "Children are wonderful perceivers and terrible interpreters." And this is so true! My very own daughter would say often about her friends, "But, Daddy, they are so nice!" Yes, this is true. Our children are going to meet, make friends, develop "best friends," and be influenced by this whole process. They will meet a lot of really nice kids in their peer groups, but as we have seen with the successful parents in our study, children need help in *maintaining balance*. These parents were there for them in this.

I am sure that you are in complete agreement with this basic principle of parenting. No doubt you have a clear understanding of what it means to become unequally yoked in relationships. It is one thing to know the principle of this kind of imbalance; it is quite a different task to facilitate this in regards to your children.

Practical applications

1. Be willing to do whatever it takes to be *in the know*! *You* are the parent! So do the following:
   a) Become "techy" if you have to.
   b) Wear a beaten path to the school.
   c) Know your neighborhood, be aware of all the movies that are showing at the local theater, and never give carte blanche approval of the families where your child is visiting or having a sleepover.
   d) Know the friends of your child at a deeper-than-surface level.
   e) Don't feel bad about being the "filter" through which all computer sites and computer time are monitored.
   f) Please remember the necessity of the following three parenting elements: *firmness, consistency,* and *follow-through.*
   g) Most importantly, please remember: *make sure that the message of love gets through.*

2. Do whatever it takes to keep the lines of communication open between you and the kids. So do the following:

   a) No taboo areas! All topics are out on the table for discussion.

   b) Consider it a compliment to you as a parent when your child reveals to you their negative feelings or emotional hurts. Just as Christians are taught in Scripture not to quench the Spirit, likewise, we are admonished in Scripture not to exasperate our children. Jesus wanted the little children to come to him; we should want our children to come to us.

   c) *Intimacy* is a communication goal with our children. There is only one route or bridge leading to intimacy, and that is dialogue. There is no greater joy than to be on the same page with our children and no greater pain than to be in the dark.

3. Quality time is a must! Please note the following perspective: (1) the husband and wife, (2) the children, (3) jobs and/or careers, and (4) everything else. Without saying, God, of course, is at the top of this family hierarchy. But quality time must be viewed in this light:

   a) The children must see that Mom and Dad are on the same page and that they love each other deeply and dearly.

b) In *unity* (the same kind of unity that Jesus prayed for his followers to have in John 17), the attention is then turned to the children. They (the children) see the love exhibited between their parents and feel loved by them.

c) The family jobs and careers are important and necessary but are secondary to the relationship between parents and children.

d) The "everything else" mentioned above is called *life*. If A, B, and C are taken care of, then life can more easily occur.

Application 2

These Successful Parents Were Big Believers in Not Only Telling Their Children What to Do and How to Live but also Were Living Examples of What They Taught.

I have often heard that you really cannot know someone until you live with them. I have had students in school who were best of friends—some throughout the whole middle school and high school years. There were occasions when these BFFs would go off to college together and as entering freshmen would choose to room together on campus. This would, in some cases, end that close friendship. We see a lot and learn a lot by living together. Children in the family setting learn from their parents what life is all about. If you have not been apprised of the term *double bind*, I need to introduce it to you here. A child who hears conflicting messages from their parents about life is being put into a double bind emotionally. A child who is punished or reprimanded for using foul language by a parent and then hears that parent use that type of language toward their spouse or even toward them concludes that "authority figures" live by a different set of rules, authority figures are hypocrites and cannot be trusted or taken seriously, or maybe the children may think that they can be dominant and mean to those younger than themselves. Again, "Children are wonderful perceivers and terrible interpreters!" Your children will learn from you how to control anger. They will learn from you what is important in life. Your children will learn from you how to treat others. Your children will learn from you about faith in God. One of the most important things your children will learn from you will be how to live with a spouse. They will learn how to be a husband or wife and how to respect a husband or wife. All these life lessons will be learned day by day right under the roofs of your houses.

I am compelled just here to include comments from one of the families in our research. You will see in these words the very application of the important principle we are discussing:

> We feel incredibly blessed that our children have turned out so well and give God the glory for that. We were very careful and deliberate when our children were growing up that we "recognized" God all along the way for his goodness, intervention, etc. Their mother never saw a sunset when

she was around the kids that she did not say, "Only God can do that." She would also do this when we were in the mountains or regarding the stars in the sky. These were small but important reminders to our children about the majesty, power, kindness, etc., of God. Our children have been exposed to perhaps more than their fair share of heartache over a relatively short time. However, through it all, we could see many blessings. They were blessed to watch their mother's dad take amazing, loving care of their grandmother who suffered from dementia for nine years. It was a lesson for all of us and for anyone who knew her parents. To watch this man love and cherish his Christian bride (and put his life on hold for nine years to give her his full attention) until she took her final breath was so beautiful. She died in 2010. In 2012, I (the father) was diagnosed with stage IV cancer (invasive carcinoma) with eight masses in my neck and head. I went through extensive chemo/radiation and had to be given a feeding tube. I contracted sepsis. My wife had to be the one to break it to our children and our parents because I just could not. We didn't know how this news would affect our children, especially spiritually, because you hear of things like this shattering someone's faith. We can only give credit to God that he did not allow it to affect their faith in a negative way. It made them stronger. This came at a very critical time in the life of one of our sons as he was just beginning his senior year. He was so strong. Our children saw their mother taking excellent care of me with faith that God would bring us through this. I told them that there was a light at the end of the tunnel either way for me. When all of it was over, our son (the HS senior) gave his mom the most meaningful gift she had ever received. It was a cross that had footprints on one side, and on the other, it simply said, "It was then that I carried you." He knew that she was only able to stay strong because of Jesus, and he knew that *she* knew that also. There are times during that very difficult period that she doesn't remember, but the kids do, and she just feels like those were the times that Jesus was completely carrying her.

[The following are the words and sentiments of the mother.] In 2013, my dad took his life. This could have been a deal-breaker of faith for any of us. However, we understood his actions, and he believed that God comes to the brokenhearted which, definitely, was my dad. A lot of people don't understand this, and you may not either; however, we have much peace about this. You see, after dealing with my mom's dementia for nine years and seeing the impact that it had on all of us, kids, grandkids, etc., Dad *knew* its effect on a family. For a few months leading up to his death, he was having heart issues and was exhibiting signs of dementia that he was all too fully aware of. His biggest fear in life was being debilitated by a stroke (like my mother's father was for two years) or burdening us with something like what our mom went through (even though we would have been honored to care for him). Anyway, heart issues were continuing. He couldn't sleep at all, and he was more and more aware of his symptoms of dementia. So on March 20, 2013, he took his life after getting all his affairs in complete order. We were devastated, but we weren't 100 percent surprised. He was lost those three years without mom, not relieved of not having to care for her like some may have been. They had been married for nearly sixty-four years. He left a note for us that was simple but to the point. It simply said, "I love you all. I miss your mother. I cannot put you all through this again. I'm asleep in the basement." I know a lot of Christians who believe that suicide is a one-way ticket to hell. Perhaps they are right. I chose not to think that way because of my dad's mental condition and because his death wasn't to punish anyone (as is the case in some suicides) or to escape something unethical. It was because he loved his family and didn't want them to suffer more or to be burdened with his care. I was a little worried about people's reactions, but ironically, a friend of mine had some words that greatly comforted me. He knew my mom and dad well and knew the remarkable care he had given my mom. When he found out from me that dad had died (and also the circumstances of his death), I expected some response like, "Oh, that's too bad," or, "How selfish of him." But instead, he responded by referring to that verse in the Bible that speaks of "laying down one's life for a brother." This is what came to his mind. He said that we usually think of that verse as for someone who dies in the military or someone who dies while trying to save someone else. He said that he viewed what my dad did was sparing his family from more long-term grief; thus, he laid down his life for us. Others may not agree, and that's okay. But God knew my dad's heart and his mental state of confusion, and I chose to believe that Dad didn't go straight to hell. Do we, his family, believe that he made the right choice? Absolutely not! But we understand his choice. The rest of my siblings and all my parent's grandchildren (including my kids) reacted to Dad's death with great faith albeit with grief, and they all spoke at his funeral. His death was not about how he *died* but how he *lived* and *loved*.

[The following now are some words and thoughts of the father.] Four months after my wife's dad's death, our children lost another grandparent when my mom died after a long battle with cancer. They again saw how the family rallies to those who are sick and suffering, and again, God did not allow the faith of our children to be shaken. We are so grateful for that.

During their teen and young adult years, our children were all affected by poor decisions being made by Christian adults and mentors in their lives. Sometimes when children are raised in a household of faith and witness respectable adult Christians make poor decisions, it can negatively affect their faith. Some adopt the mindset that these shortcomings indicate that Christians are primarily hypocrites. Many Christians leave the church over such things. Realizing those viewpoints, we were prayerful when the Christians we knew personally made poor choices that had reverberating consequences. We discussed these situations with our kids, explaining that we are all sinners and fall short but that we are forgiven by God who loves us and gives us second chances. These were also lessons exemplifying why we should put our trust only in God because people will let us down. Some situations angered our children and left them feeling deceived by those they respected, but they somehow managed to love and forgive, realizing they would hope for the same mercy if and when they ever needed it. Again, we are thankful that God guarded their hearts and minds throughout these situations because any of them could have resulted in unhealthy anger, resentment, lack of forgiveness, or wavering of their faith since not even "good" Christians can live as they should.

Finally, my wife's near-death illness this past November could have also shattered the faith of our children. The surgeon said that if it had gone on two more hours, she would not have made it due to all the infection. She and I missed Thanksgiving with our family as she was hospitalized from November 18 until November 30 and then rehospitalized a couple of weeks after that.

She missed the birth of our grandson. She had been in the room during the birth of our daughter's other two children and had the blessing of cutting their cords. She missed the grandson's birth completely and also could not take care of our daughter for two weeks as she had done before. This was devastating for her, but she chose to focus on the thanksgiving of God's intervention and all the ways he revealed himself throughout the ordeal. Being left with a colostomy was also devastating, but thankfully, it was reversed at the end of February, and she recovered well. As it turns out, all of what happened to her was the result of a colonoscopy in which the doctor perforated her colon. The leakage of toxins from that perforation into her abdominal cavity for two weeks before her hospitalization was what nearly killed her. This time, the shoe was on the other foot. I had to take care of her completely for two months. She couldn't do anything for herself. She lost thirty-two pounds and had great difficulty recovering. Now we have both faced and overcome life-threatening situations, and our kids have witnessed God at work through all of it, and they have seen our faith remain steadfast throughout. We are very, very thankful that none of these events negatively affected our children's faith. *To God be the glory!*"

Practical applications

1. Parents, *get your act together!* This is the same plea that Jesus made in his prayer to the Father in John 17. He prayed,

   My prayer is not for them [his disciples] alone. I pray also for those who will believe in me through their message, that all of them may be one, Father, just as you are in me and I am in you. May they also be one in us *so that the world may believe that you have sent me.* (John 17:20–22; emphasis added)

Jesus was praying that the disciples would *get their act together!* Why? *So that the world would believe!* This is precisely the point here. As parents, we must realize that conflicting messages to our children result in nonbelievers. When I say "nonbelievers," it does not just apply to spiritual matters. Of course, spiritual matters are most important; however, any principle that you do not emulate before your children will not carry much weight in the long run.

2. Keep in mind the principle of spiritual attrition. The unity principle of John 17 discussed above is a sure deterrent to spiritual attrition or the loss of faith among second-generation offspring. Spiritual attrition in families is a slow process. The flames of this type of faith digression are fueled by parents with very little spiritual backbone who are afraid to make the daily decisions of spiritual leadership in the home and who allow Satan's world to come right in and inhabit the social media, bedrooms, recreation and entertainment areas, and even kitchen and cupboard. This leads to practical application principle number 2, which is *commitment!* "As for me and my house, we will serve the Lord" (Josh. 24:15). What your children need to see with this commitment is a trait we see in our Lord: "the same yesterday, today, and forever." When they see that we are committed to serving the Lord, that we love him *and* them, and that they can count on us daily (yesterday, today, and forever), most likely they will not join the ranks of the lost "second generation."

3. There appeared to be something very special that these families possessed that a lot of families do not have. I am speaking here of an "intangible" quality, something that was not announced or proclaimed in any specific way but was sensed throughout the whole family. It was an attribute that every member of the family recognized as inherent in "our" family. This is who we are. This is what we are all about. This is what we do. The whole family was involved. The whole family had a place, a part, and felt both needed and accepted because of it. It also served to be the glue that held the family together. There might be many words that would describe this entity; however, the word I would apply here would be *values*. Yes, they had values that served to be the very fiber of their existence as a family. These values helped the children to have feelings of security and trust in their parents. A common bond was more easily developed over time as they not only saw what their parents did but also they practiced these family values alongside them. It may have been their faith and involvement in their Christian walk. It may have been their involvement in sports or their love of a professional or college team. It could possibly have been their love of camping, fishing, or hunting. Rather than something specific like this,

it may have been their heavy involvement in the family itself (i.e., holidays, visits, trips, and get-togethers). The concept to hold onto here is *family values*.

Following are some of the families that participated in this family research. I asked them to include a short biographical sketch to give us a glimpse into their lives and what was most important to them. I hope you appreciate the pictures and the thoughts expressed as much as I do.

On June 4, 2020, we will celebrate 49 years of marriage. Our life together has blessed us with a son who serves as a deacon and a daughter who teaches Bible classes. We also have four wonderful grandsons, a daughter-in-law and a son-in-law. We love to eat together and play games when everyone can come visit us! Our most special family time is at Christmas. We are blessed to have responsible and faithful children.

Christ is the center of our family, and faith in him is the foundation on which our family was built. We are blessed with rich heritages of faith, family, love and discipline that we deliberately fostered in our children. Our family is very close. We love each other deeply, celebrate the joys of life richly, cherish family ties devotedly, enjoy family traditions deliberately, have fun regularly and communicate constantly. As a family, we love sports, dogs, holidays, the mountains, the beach, playing games, America, the Tennessee Titans, politics and SEC football. We DO have lively bantering during football season since the Georgia Bulldogs, Florida Gators and Tennessee Vols are represented in our family, but at the end of the day, we all love God, each other and the SEC.

The Ashberry family began in 2002. We began our family later in life, according to our world's view. Sean and I were married "old". He was 32 and I was 29. As we began to plan to add to our family, we hit a speed bump due to infertility issues. We began infertility treatments in 2004 and were blessed by the birth of our oldest child in 2006. God continued to bless with the birth of our daughter in 2008, and then our youngest son in 2009. We went from not knowing if we could have children to three in a span of 27 months. We learned from the experience to enjoy each moment and each milestone with our kids, and that God' timing is always perfect.

We tried to focus on family time and keeping the children involved in their youth group at church. Their friends were of likeminded faith. Their youth group was very close; they did things together and outside the organized church activities.

"Originally, we were a family of four children; three boys and one girl. We have grown to be a much bigger family. All the children have married and have given us six grandchildren with another on the way at this time. The first grandchild was a girl, after which we have had a run of all boys. We love the outdoors, the beach, the mountains and just spending time together. An interesting note: Our children all have spouses that come from good home lives and from parents who are still married. Their in laws have been married from 33 to 45 years."

Our family was built on core beliefs that center around
faith, love and friendship. Open discussions, humor and
affection were normal in our home. We both are in helping
professions, so it was central for us to teach the boys to be
generous and compassionate, as life is not always fair. We
stressed that money is not important, but what you do with
what you have is important. There will always be people who
have more and are smarter, etc., but God made each one of
us special in our own way, so be humble, work hard and treat
everyone with respect. Christian friendships were encouraged
as well as developing their own faith, along with a sense of
God' plan for them as individuals. No family lived close so
we adopted fellow Christians as "grandparents" who were role
models for our boys. We were blessed to have our boys attend
and graduate from a Christian school and continue a family
tradition when they graduated from Lipscomb University.

When our family was created over 40 years ago, we did not have a DIY book to lay things out step by step. As we started writing our love story, the bar was high, as we were coming from generations of single marriages and Christian homes. We relied on prayer and the Bible and its teachings, as had the generation before us, to grant us values and principles by which to live. We incorporated its truths in our decision making and these became the anchor of our family life. Our family was an ineffable blessing and our greatest responsibility. With God at the center, church and Christian school were our supports. We did not allow peer pressures or popular trends to outweigh our commitment to training our children according to the teachings of God. Worshipping together brought our family together and kept us grounded I. What would be the cornerstone of our existence as the "Cole" family. We valued our "together": playing together, working together, laughing together, eating together and intensely enjoying being together. Looking back, there are a few trademarks that bounded our family together, heart and soul:

1. God was the center; we" lived and breathed it; nothing came before it.
2. As parents, we pledged to present a united front in our decisions. This brought solidarity, respect, love and trust to our family.
3. We agreed that it was our responsibility to raise/train our children; not the church; not the school; not other friends.
4. We had a little phrase that meant a lot to us: Be your best self at all times because the best will expect nothing less.
5. We always had a standard reply when our children tried the, "Well, so-n-so is doing it!" The Cole rule is, "We are only responsible for you."
6. Laughter was always the best medicine.
7. We trained them to be team players with several hearts: at home, at church, at school, on mission trips, at camp, at sports, in careers and in life.
8. Prayer was taught and modeled early to imprint on our children's hearts and minds the one source of all their strength and wisdom.
9. Did I mention that the tie that binds and seals our family together is our love and obedience to God.
10. We were never perfect, but it was our imperfections that provided the opportunities to live with trust and reliance on God before our children.

Application 3

The Successful Parents in This Study Believed in the Principle of Hard Work. They Required Chores to Be Done at Home, and They Encouraged Their Children to Work at Part-Time Jobs Outside the Home.

Many parents practice the philosophy of, "It's just easier to do it yourself." No truer statement could be made because it *is* easier to do it yourself, and what is more, you can do a much better job by *yourself!* We all know that is not the point. Another truism in this matter is, "I can get it done a lot quicker." Yes, you can get the job done a lot quicker. Allow your mind to escape to an earlier time in our history, to a time when life appeared to be a lot simpler, to the days of your grandparents or even great grandparents. For the most part, this was a time when children did a lot of on-the-job training in the home. If they had eggs on the table for breakfast, it was because one of the children went to the henhouse to fetch them. If there was water to drink, it was because a child drew it from the well. If there was milk to drink, one of the kids had gone in the barn to milk the cows. I am sure you are getting the picture, and probably for many of you, this was something you saw on *Little House on the Prairie*. I am sure you are also saying that you do not own a cow, nor do you have a well in your back yard. The successful parents in this study did not have those things either, but they must have understood the very important parenting principle of hard work and taking ownership of the family to which they belonged. There is a huge difference between being a spectator and being a player. One thing that must be taken into consideration here is that children (zero to eighteen) are wonderful *perceivers* but terrible *interpreters!* The more your children are permitted to be part of family rituals and obligations, the better they will be at making better and healthier interpretations about life. Finding ways to bring back the principles of hard work in the family setting are what the families in this research found across the board that produced the great kids they sent out into the schools, the church, and the world. I also noticed that these families encouraged their children to have part-time jobs in the workplace in their communities. Paul expressed a valuable principle in his letter to Timothy in 1 Timothy 6:1–2 that we, as parents, must practice in our work relationships but one that we must help our children to learn and practice also. He said that some of the bosses we have are not going to be fair or may even be mean. Paul emphasized the "respectful approach" to them, no matter how they may operate their business. How will our children ever be able to learn this extremely valuable lesson of respect if they are not actually *in* the workplace? In the above text, Paul concluded his remarks by saying, "This is what you must teach and tell everyone to do." I would say, then, "This is what we must teach and tell our children to do." I would make one more observation: it is such an exhilarating feeling for a young person to work at a job and get a paycheck and to have his/her own money. To use this money to purchase, save, contribute, and help in finances around the home is the process of independence at work. The families in our research did not deprive their children of this opportunity.

Practical applications

What a great principle! What a logical and common-sense principle, but what a difficult principle to incorporate in today's world. How easy it is to bring up objections, "We both work, and by the time we get home in the evenings, it is all we can do just to make it to bedtime and then start all over again."

You may be caught up in the "millennial mayhem," as I call it. You may or may not consider yourself a millennial; however, you still may find yourself hopelessly entangled. Commonly, what we see is a couple in their twenties to early forties with two or more children, both work outside the home. This is usually a necessity since very rarely will one income allow this couple to make financial ends meet. One or more of the children will be in the nursery or day care (adding to the financial woes), and the retrieval process begins after work in the afternoons. Then begins "circus number one"—supper, baths, homework, children's issues, and any other unannounced surprises. Following these rituals comes "circus number two"! Once the kids are in bed, there is not much time left for any quality conversation or bonding time for Mom and Dad. They are usually so tired after all the day's turmoil that the only thing left to do is go to bed and start it all over again the next day. This scenario varies somewhat from household to household and couple to couple, but I think you get the point. And sadly, many of you can truly relate. Sadly too, there are thousands of families throughout our country that are caught up in this web of confusion *and do not even know it!* They think it is the American way. The results of this type of lifestyle—if we can call it a lifestyle—are tragic. The following are just a few of those results: marital discord and, many times, divorce; stress and anxiety, both in parents and children; unnecessary medication habits; infidelity; child misbehavior; and the list can go on and on.

You may be wondering what millennial mayhem has to do with the principle of providing for work opportunities both in the home and outside the home. Some of the successful families we surveyed were very busy people. Many of them were families in which both parents held jobs outside the home (about 75%). There appeared to be a value that most of these families possessed that enabled them to deal with millennial mayhem, and that was to help their children build a strong sense of self-reliance. What better way to bring this about than to give them the opportunities to participate, work, engage, and actually *be* a responsible part of the family rather than a mere spectator to be cared for. With this in mind, consider the following practical applications:

1. Make sure the message of love gets through!
2. Children ages zero to six are very concrete in their thinking, and they need a lot of rituals and traditions. They need to get up in the morning at the same time, eat at the same time, follow the same schedule as much as possible, evening rituals, and going to bed at the same time and the same way.
3. Children ages seven to twelve need all of the above. Plus, parents need to realize that contextual thinking begins around ages seven or eight, so parenting approaches need to change. They are capable of "conceptual thinking," and they need to be weaned off with so much concrete thinking approaches.
4. As early as possible, create and allow choices for children. Present them with two or three choices (each one being acceptable to you), and let them decide.
5. Take the time to teach "leaving their area cleaner than they found it." This is an old philosophy

I practiced with the teams I coached; we would have to leave the visiting dugout cleaner than when we walked in. Early on, children must learn to clean up their messes.

6. As soon as possible, allow children to participate in preparation for the family meal at suppertime. (You may be thinking, What is that?) Two things are missing from most homes these days, and they are suppertime and front porches. I can't expect you to add a front porch to your house, but I don't feel bad at all about encouraging you and your family to institute suppertime (if you are not already) and to do it right away.

7. Please remember that *failures are excellent opportunities for growth*.

8. Parents, make up your minds together about allowances and rewards for jobs done around the house (only 30% of our surveyed families practiced this), but as soon as possible, *create* opportunities for them to participate *with you* in taking care of the home front. *They need to take ownership of their own family!*

Application 4

The Successful Families in This Research Were Open with Their Children by Allowing Them the "Freedom to Be Me." More Particularly, Their Children Felt Free to Express Themselves and to Have an Opinion. Along with This, These Children Were Allowed to Fail Knowing It Is Okay to Experience Failure. Failure Brings with It Consequences, and These Parents Helped in Creating a Consequential Environment.

Here are some of the quotes:

- "We were open and honest with them, whether the topic was good or bad. They knew they were loved unconditionally."
- "Each of our children was unique, so we focused on his or her uniqueness. We gave both positive and negative criticism, and no disrespect was ever tolerated."

- "We tried to get them to see every situation from another's point of view."
- "We were strict but loving. We expected them to live by family rules. Consequences were inevitable, and in all situations, *love!*"
- "We allowed our children to try new things and face the consequences. We would support them no matter what the outcome was."
- "We had conversations on how things could have been done better so there could be a better game plan next time."
- "We always welcomed discussion at the dinner table; while praying at night; riding in the car; or at weekly family meetings, discussing plans, schedules, and other necessary topics. We invited their opinions. They knew we loved them because they heard it every day."
- "We validated them and guided them without judgment."
- "We were old school. We felt there were some things that children and parents don't discuss. We were more of their parent than their friend. We never instilled blame, shame, or guilt. We never dumped on them."
- "They knew they could talk to us about anything, and we would not embarrass them. We would neither judge them nor condemn them nor betray their confidence in us. We would

share everyday things, things said or done during the day."

- "Nothing was off-limits, and we loved them, no matter what."
- "We always told them that they could talk to us about anything."
- "By the time our kids were of the age of understanding, they knew our expectations. Treat people with respect; don't use bad language; don't speak derogatorily of anyone; respect your teachers; study hard, and get a college education; be in church, and take part; and boys treat young ladies with respect, and girls act respectfully. Our kids were not perfect. They made many mistakes, but they knew we were there for them when they failed."
- "We always allowed them to experience the consequences of their mistakes, no matter how badly we wanted to alleviate it for them."
- "We tried to be consistent with our discipline. We did not just threaten. We followed through with discipline."

I am not sure what you picked up from these quotes, but four words come to mind for me: openness, choices, consequences, and respect. Your children are younger than you, but that does not make them any less of a person than you. They have the same needs that you have to not only survive but also succeed in this life. Often, as adults, we tend to treat those younger than us as though we possess a higher level of intelligence and that we are deserving of more respect than they do. Before you totally leave me on this, please hear me out. Intelligence is a gift from God. The young and old alike have it, and the only thing that age does is to give one experience in how to use that intelligence. I do not want to get into the IQ debate or discussion but only to say that there is a distinct possibility that your or my child could very well be more intelligent than we are! But like I said, this is not about intelligence. It is more about parents realizing that we are dealing with a true gift from God, a living, breathing human being full of potential and deserving of all the nurture a mom and dad can give. Need I turn our minds to Paul's words in Ephesians 6:4, "Fathers, do not provoke your children to anger, but bring them up in the discipline and instruction of the Lord."

Just a sidelight here from my experience with children. This mainly comes from the educational experiences I have been blessed to have with all those parents who, for the most part, blessed me with the opportunity to work and learn from their children as I taught them in the classroom and coached them on the ball field. You may agree with this, or you have the obvious right to disagree. *There is absolutely no correlation or link between morality and intelligence*! I have noticed in more cases than I can count or even recall that the child who is blessed with a high degree of intelligence displays some or all of the following:

1. Laziness (It comes too easy for them, and they never develop a work ethic.)

2. Craftiness (They become better at conniving and finding ways to buck the system.)
3. Haughtiness (Many tend to look down on those who are a little slower academically.)
4. Entitlement (A lot of teachers love to work with the students who get it the first time around and are easy to teach, which results sometimes in the teacher-pet syndrome.)

Back to the original statement regarding the lack of a link between morality and intelligence. Your children have the basic need to be loved *unconditionally*. Not only do they have this need, but they also need to have someone to love. Here is where we, parents, come into the picture. *Our emotional and spiritual needs far outweigh our intellectual needs!* In fact, I would go so far as to say that if the emotional needs are not met, there is no amount of intelligence in a child's head that will guide him/her safely through the "moral storms" that they will have to endure, especially in their teenage years and early twenties.

Thanks for bearing with me on this little excursion. Now with these considerations in mind, think about the four takeaways from the comments of the parents in this research: *openness, choices, consequences,* and *respect.*

Openness. This is a concept that is key to our obtaining intimacy with our children. This may sound like a rather strange statement to make in this context; however, it is very fitting. So many children grow up like strangers in their homes, not ever feeling included and not ever feeling free to share with their parents. Did you ever stop to think that maybe the reason for this might be that as parents, very little effort or time is being put toward achieving intimacy with our children? By intimacy, I am talking about being on the same page. I am talking about being approachable. I am talking about being *vulnerable*! Yes, I used the correct word here. The higher the level of vulnerability in the parent-child relationship, the higher the level of intimacy will be achieved. By being open, real, and willing to admit our mess-ups, we show our children that they can be *open, real,* and *willing to admit their mess-ups.*

Choices. There is a valuable lesson that parents of young children need to learn very early on, and that is power in *choice.* I would go so far as to say that if this lesson is not learned, both the parent and the child are in for very tough days ahead. There is great value in the following wording to a young child, "Which of these three would you like to wear today?" as opposed to, "Here, this is what you are wearing today!" Capability is to be ingrained in children, and one of the greatest parental tools is *choice.* But this is not a parenting tool for young children only. As they grow and mature mentally, emotionally, physically and, especially, spiritually, the tool of *choice* becomes the catalyst for maturity in each of these areas. It is a shame that as children grow older, they are not allowed to gradually take appropriate ownership in their lives; and much to their disappointment later, some parents don't allow this. Their logic may be that they don't want to give up the control or that they are afraid their children will make mistakes or even because of a strange view they have of love that they want their children to stay dependent on them. Choice was definitely one of the major tools in the hands of the parents in this research.

Consequences. One of the leading causes of low self-esteem and the tragic mindset of incapability is for a child to grow up being sheltered from experiencing the consequences of their bad decisions. It should go without saying that I am not speaking here of the normal and logical protection that parents give their children when they are in harm's way. I have in mind here the day-to-day decisions a child may make such as going outside when it is cold without a jacket. A lot of parents would not think of allowing such. Hopefully, the child goes outside, sees that it is cold, and then returns inside to get a jacket. This may appear minor, but when this becomes our mode of operation, our children learn from "natural consequences," and they begin learning to take care of themselves. Just one other little insight here: *mistakes are great opportunities for growth!* We, as parents, need to learn to allow mistakes and, along with those mistakes, to make sure our children are allowed to learn from them. Our research study shows that parents saw the importance of consequences in their parenting process.

Respect. If there is one area of lament as far as parental gripes in our world today, it is that young people do not respect their parents or, for that matter, adults in general. Yes, when I was coming up (in the deep South), "Yes/No, sir/ma'am" was the order of the day along with many other words and phrases depicting respect. Of course, my friends up North would argue this point, saying that a respectful yes or no was just as acceptable, and this was probably true. There is one language of respect regardless of where you grew up, and that was that if you *give* respect, you will have a lot better chance of *receiving* respect! This, by the way, is a great parenting tool. I have seen and heard parents who speak to and treat their children with the utmost *disrespect* and then expect them to respond with respect. This brings up another detrimental action in the parenting process, and that is parents who treat their children this way put their children into a *double bind* in the parent-child relationship. A double bind is created when a child is treated disrespectfully (which is usually without a show of love) and then is expected to *love* and *respect* that parent. If your mind is going where mine is going on this, you readily and accurately interpret this as *emotional abuse*. Again, this references what Paul wrote in Ephesians 6, showing that he evidently knew the importance of avoiding this dilemma, "Fathers, do not provoke your children to anger, but bring them up in the discipline and instruction of the Lord."

Practical applications

1. Using your own wisdom, and knowing your child as you do, start early providing choices.
2. Allow for failure, realizing that without failure, there will be no real learning.
3. Allow for "natural consequences" more than setting up "logical consequences" in your child's learning environment.
4. Make sure you impress upon your child early on what the family's value system entails. There is some leeway that may be given when a child messes up in some areas; however, when a child disregards a family value, he/she needs to understand the gravity of that choice.
5. Remember three extremely important parenting principles: be firm, be consistent, and follow through.
6. An important concept to get across to a child is that they live in a loving home with loving parents and that they serve a loving God. This being the case, they will not be treated as criminals or *animals*. I know this sounds rather brash that I would make this statement; however, some parents, without realizing it, do this very thing. I will mention three words that come into play here: *related, respectful,* and *reasonable*. With criminals and animals, these words seldom come into play. A criminal is treated

with disrespect, usually because he has lost his right to basic respect; he is forced and commanded to be subject to rules with very little love lost in the process. An animal is taught to sit, roll over, or fetch with the use of positive or negative reinforcement. Hopefully, there is not a parent out there who would ascribe to any of these tactics in training their children, *but we do*! Using the three words mentioned above (related, respectful, and reasonable), parents assure their children that they are living in a loving home, that they themselves are loving parents, and that we all serve a loving God. When the discipline we administer fits each of these criteria, we accomplish these goals. When I, as a parent, *relate* the consequence to the infraction, I am assuring them that they brought this on themselves. I did not just pull something out of the air to throw on them (as a criminal might be treated). When I react with *respectfulness* to their infraction and do not treat them as though they are stupid, dumb, or not very intelligent, I am assuring them that they are loved and that there is nothing they can ever do that will endanger their place as a child in this family. And finally, when I, as a parent, am *reasonable* in my administration of discipline, I do not discourage them to the point that they feel there is no way to ever work themselves back into our good graces. Steven Glenn, in his book *Raising Self Reliant Children in a Self-indulgent World*, describes a scenario in which a child that they had taken into their home from an abusive family setting had decided one day, upon returning home from school, to crank up the family car sitting in the driveway. Somehow, he managed to shift into drive, and the car lunged forward, taking out the garage door and ramming into the back wall leading out to the back yard. He was devastated and ran immediately to hide. Upon returning home, Steven saw what had happened and began searching for his son. Upon finding him hiding, the boy explained what happened and also described his fear of being sent out of his new home. Mr. Glenn compassionately let him know that he was no longer living in a "temporary" home; he was living in a home with a family and that there was nothing he could ever do that would jeopardize his place in this family. He did go on to say that the boy would certainly have a part in paying the consequences of his blunder. He said, "We used to have a garage. Now we have a carport, and you will have your part in its restoration and repair." This young man emerged from this incident feeling loved, accepted, respected, and responsible.

Application 5

The Successful Parents in This Research Were Addictive-Free to Alcohol, Drugs, and Tobacco. It Began at the Top (With the Parents) and Was Followed by the Expectation of High Moral Values in the Lives of Their Children on These Substances.

The principle here is clean living. I am not intending here to debate the issue of abstinence from alcohol or drugs or tobacco; I am just saying that in 100% of these families, there was no alcohol or drugs used at all. In 91% of these families, there was no use of tobacco. To take it one step farther, it was even noted that in 55% of these families, there were no members of their extended families who used any of these substances. Please keep in mind that the purpose of this study was to find out what successful parents did that facilitated them in getting the results they achieved. I, like you, certainly realize that it is not so much what one does *not* do that brings about success; it is more about what one *does*. Certainly, God's

Word is a *positive* book that shows and tells us his desires for our lives. We all know of those we would label as hypocrites who say one thing yet do another. All of this being said, it is hard to ignore Paul's list of the fruits of the Spirit and the works of the flesh in Galatians 5. Works of the flesh include sexual immorality, impurity, sensuality, idolatry, sorcery, enmity, strife, jealousy, fits of anger, rivalries, dissensions, divisions, envy, drunkenness, orgies, and things like these. The fruits of the Spirit are love, joy, peace, patience, kindness, goodness, faithfulness, gentleness, and self-control.

Practical applications

1. If I had to be limited to only one practical application in this area, it would be this: *practice what you preach*! When I worked with a little church in a rural area, I was approached by one of the families about their son who was about fifteen years of age. They said that they had caught him smoking and that they wanted me to talk to him. In talking with him, I discovered that his father was a smoker. He never brought his cigarettes inside the house; he did his smoking outside. Needless to say, I did not get too far with this young man. There is nothing more powerful in guiding children to do the right thing than *a godly example*.

2. Develop and extend trust (in that order). We have already discussed the power of choice; that applies in this discussion. Once we have developed trust with our children, then we will be able to give them some rope but *never enough rope to hang themselves!* Remember that trust always involves *risk*, and where there is risk, there is the possibility that your child will mess up.

3. Always know their friends, and please, please know that *you are their parent, not their friend.*

4. Create an atmosphere in which your child or children know that they can call you any time they find themselves in a situation they cannot handle or in which they feel very uncomfortable and know that you will gladly come and pick them up.

Application 6

The Successful Parents in Our Study Spent Quality Time with Their Children. If There Was More Than One Child in the Family, Each Child Received Quality Time from the Parents. Another Way to Put This Is to Say That Each Child Received Their Parent's Undivided Attention.

The following are some of the comments they made:

1. "We took the time to try and be clearer about their decisions rather than taking things for granted."
2. "We realized the importance of quality time."
3. "On days off, we would try to have fun with the kids rather than do a lot of chores. We would always try and have devotional time with them."
4. "We tried to relax more and enjoy with the children."
5. "We took vacations."

6. "Our quality time was around the dinner table. We ate dinner at the table every night."

7. "We ate together as a family. We had evening devotions. When we traveled, we would usually sing together. We had the same vacation spots that we all liked a lot."

8. "We took yearly vacations and visited the grandparents at Thanksgiving and Christmas. We would always go look at the lights at Christmas. We took trips to the mountains in the fall. The kids had dogs. We loved certain movies and TV shows. College football was a favorite of ours."

Discipline, education, and chores are important family matters; however, some other matters are just as important, if not more, and that is the family cohesion that is created through the quality time shared by parents and children. The following scriptural logic may appear to you as somewhat out of context, but I want to bring to your memory a statement from Jesus in John 4:24 where he said (emphasis added), "God is Spirit, and his worshippers must worship him in *Spirit* and in *truth*." Many Christians and churches are big on the "truth" part but not so big on the "Spirit" part. I want to know, though, if you caught the first part of that statement by our Lord, "God *is* Spirit!" the context of this statement bears much more heavily on the Spirit than the truth. The Samaritan woman in this text was all wrapped up in the traditional views of the religion of the day and the customs associated with all that. Jesus came into her life and stressed something that goes much deeper than facts and figures (not to say that these things are not important), and that is the spirit part of us, the emotional part of us.

Now back to the matter of discussion. We must get in touch with the emotional side of our children. We must leave with them messages of both spirit and truth. We must step out of our authoritarian mode and go deep into supplying their emotional needs. It cannot be overstated that we must make sure that the message of love gets across. What better way to do this than to "become a child with them," laugh with them, listen to them, cry with them, and just be there for them in their life issues, small and large. I need to emphasize one other important parenting principle that applies here, and that is the tragedy of unmet emotional needs. Again, remember that children are excellent perceivers and terrible interpreters. This means to us as parents that there are a lot of things in which we do not have control, and our children's perceptions are one of those things. This further emphasizes the need for practicing undivided attention with each child. If a child's perception is that he/she is not loved or accepted; that they really do not count; or that their views, questions, and everyday concerns are not important, they begin to develop what eventually turns into those *unmet emotional needs* of which I speak. Every child is different, thus displays this state of emotions differently. It is something that develops slowly yet *deliberately*! If it is not detected early on, it begins to show its ugly self during the teen years. I must share with you something that has become very evident to me as I have been dealing professionally with marital infidelity over the past few years. Much of it is a result of a feeling of unmet emotional needs. On the male side of things, I have seen a striking common thread among a very high percentage of husbands who have turned to pornography or extramarital relationships and that most of them discovered pornographic materials around the ages of twelve to fourteen, the very exact time that mothers and fathers need to be coming on very strong with the validation in their lives that they *belong*, that they are *accepted*, that they are *loved*, and that they hold a very valuable place in their family. This type of reinforcement will help in protecting them from the onslaught of Satan through movies, magazines, and other media that portray pornography and other means of illicit sexual involvement as a "normal" outlet for their newfound sexual urges. This is exactly how Satan works in this world; this is how he gets his foot in the door of vulnerable children. This type of literature and photography sends a false message of love (eros) to children who are searching for something to fill the emotional gap inside. Without going into the inevitable path that this opens, it will suffice to emphasize the importance of making sure your children *know* they are loved. What better way to do this than through extending to them genuine quality love every day of the week through quality time in the form of physical presence, concerns for their concerns, and just taking time to *be* with them one-on-one.

Practical applications

There was a study undertaken way back in the '70s that I believe still has ramifications for families today. In this study, six thousand teens (twelve to eighteen years old) were posed with a question that had four possible answers: Were your families close, somewhat close, not too close, or not close at all? The analysis of these kids showed that those who answered, "Not close at all," also reported that they weren't happy most of the time, felt life was boring, liked to do things to shock people, felt they had less fun than most people, seldom felt close to people, didn't care about their grades in school, were not concerned about getting along with their parents, were not concerned about living up to their moral and religious training, felt they were not getting a good education, and didn't expect to go to college (Glenn 210).

Consider the following practical applications:

1. Parents and children *share mutual worlds*. (I have actually talked to students who did not even know their parent's occupation.) Not only should you be aware of what is going on in your child's daily life, but your child should also be aware of what is going on in your daily life.

2. Use "specific" rather than "general" praise. Examples are, "I like the way you said that!" "Those are great colors you chose!" "I really appreciate your work ethic in this class." "I see how you could feel that way!" These are all specific statements that show recognition for the child rather than a mere, "Great job!" or "That's nice." Specific praise gives attention to the child rather than the project they are working on.

3. Pay close attention to your child's body language. Without being overly and "parentally" intrusive, try to find out what is going on in their world.

4. Be present for their activities (this goes without saying).

5. This next practical application needs to be applied with a lot of care: parents need to "tiptoe" carefully. Let your child know that you always are on their team and that you have their back. This is very difficult when they are not on the right path, when they have messed up, and when they are in trouble at school. If you abandon them and fully take the side of the accuser, the school, or the other person, *you have just lost your influence.* This is the time for you to express not your disdain for their bad decision (at least not at first) but to relay to them how badly it makes *you* feel and how

disappointed *you* are inside that your child has made this bad decision. This is one of the most critical times for you to *make sure that the message of love* gets across. To use a very trite statement, "Your child is not a bad child. He/she did a bad thing!"

6. Remember family values. There is no greater feeling than that of "ownership," and that is what we want our children to embrace. Ownership and investment into any organization or, in this case, a family is dependent upon the members buying into the makeup, the nature, and the direction of the group. This involves the principles or values upon which it is built. In some way, parents should get these values across to the children. Children soon learn what they are and respond by saying things like, "This is what we do!" "This is where we go." "This is how we did that." The operative word is *we*. This is also very helpful to the parents when the children "buy in" to the family value system because they are no longer majoring in minors or making mountains out of molehills. The things they give attention to for the most part are when a child violates a family value system. Most other things are considered minor and are handled as such. Some things are absolutely necessary to our survival as a family, and some things are not absolutely

necessary but are still important. Parents, *pray for wisdom and patience!* The following are some examples of family values. Some may be yours, some may not be:

a) Spirituality
b) Our American heritage
c) Music
d) Sports
e) Education
f) Camping, fishing, and hunting
g) Art
h) Drama
i) Horses
j) Farming

Application 7

Ninety-Seven Percent of the Successful Families in This Research Had Children Who Participated in Athletics.

I don't know where your thoughts are going on this. I hope you are not bewildered, thinking that you need to make sure your child becomes an athlete of some sort at some level. This is not the point! Yes, I am a coach. Yes, I played as an athlete at the high school and college level, but I am not going to conclude here that all children should be athletes and participate at some level to be successful in life. There were many questions asked in this research that covered many areas; it just so happened that athletic participation received a very high rating with the successful parents in this study. Since it did score so highly in this study, I began to think about some of the things I saw in my coaching years that might be considered as *lessons from the field of play*. Also, keep in mind that there are many other ways of achieving the results that athletic participation brings. Indeed, the main tragedy of athletic participation is that in so many families, the focus is turned to the sport itself rather than the purpose of the child's participation. We have discussed family values; family values become the filter through which all activities must pass. Parents must constantly be looking at every participation request of the child to determine whether that activity contributes to or detracts from the direction the family is going. Not only must the child's request go through this process, but also the parents themselves sometimes get caught up in the glitter of worldly pursuits, especially when their child *appears* to be on the road to being the next Babe Ruth, Michael Jordan, Tom Brady, Chris Evert, or any other great name in sports achievement. It does not matter what the endeavor is. Music, arts, sports, debate, drama, robotics, or the filter through which they pass determines what our children take with them.

Just another thought or two before we look at some practical applications. Do you remember those days when your children would get so engrossed in their play? It might have been their dolls, their toy soldiers or, as I have seen in the past, they might have been "playing church" or "playing cowboys and Indians." They may have been playing "kitchen" and cooking on their play stoves. They may have been out in the yard after rain and were making mudpies. Whatever the games or the fantasies, they were in their play world, and that was very meaningful to them. Any child therapist will tell you that this is a healthy activity. There is a whole area of child psychology devoted to playing called play therapy. There is great value in allowing children to go into their world of imagination and release emotions like this. As parents, our world is to take care of our children, provide for them, make sure they are fed and clothed, and provide security for them. Their world, especially early on, is *playing*. Where I am going with this is that parents need to provide for their children a safe and healthy play world. This would be places of acceptable emotional outlet. It might be in an activity, it might be in coloring books, and it could be in games. But for a child to have age-appropriate, parentally guided activities are *huge* in their growing-up years. This brings up a scripture reference that we have heard hundreds of times in various contexts: "Train up a child in the way he should go, and when he is old he will not depart from it" (Prov. 22:6). How often we have heard that this verse means that if we train up kids to go to church and be good, when they get older, they will not depart. Certainly, training children to go to church and make good, moral choices are great parental things to do; however, you and I have seen many children who were brought up to go to church and make good choices go off into some really dark areas of life and some never to return. I love the English Standard Version of this verse that reads, "Train up a child in the way he should go." What I take from this is that parents are to know their children so well that they understand who and what they are and then aid them to go in the ways of their strengths. We present to them opportunities for growth in the innate God-given strengths *they* have as opposed to the ways *we* might wish they will go. Of course, it is understood that we are speaking of talents that fit into the areas of intellect, physical capabilities, the arts, and such. All of us are made in the image of God; thus, all have the God-given destiny to return to him. Therefore it is also every parent's responsibility and privilege to guide their children toward God. With all this said, regardless of the type of activity (sports, arts, or something else), our children need these. As parents, we come alongside them, helping them through and making sure they stay on track with what is truly important. With all this said, the following are some practical applications that may be helpful:

Practical applications

1. Your children are constantly watching you. They can see what is important to you through your involvement, through your body language, and your intensity. Be careful of the message you are sending.

2. *Respect for authority* is a principle learned through participation in outside activities. Be very careful how you speak about your children's coach or sponsor in front of them. I can guarantee you that it will spill over into the player-coach relationship at some point. It actually works both ways. If *you* speak positively about

their coach, *they* will react respectfully toward them. What a great opportunity for your children to learn to show respect toward adults other than their parents. It starts with you as their parent.

3. *Anger and stress control* is a lesson all children need to learn. Through participation in athletics or other activities outside the home and family, they will reach points where they are pushed to the limits. To use this state of mind to move toward the goal is great; to use this state of mind to attack others or their coach is regretful. I was not primarily a basketball coach; however, I did coach the JV team at our school for a time, and I remember one game in which my main player was getting frustrated at the referee and a player on the other team. I called a time-out and told him, "Just put the ball in the hole!" I think this a great parenting principle.

4. Have a *healthy competitive spirit.* Scripture teaches us not to do anything half-heartedly. Colossians 3:23 states (emphasis added), "Whatever you do, *work heartily*, as for the Lord and not for men." There are two things here. First of all, there is the "work heartily" part. What a great place for athletics or any other school or recreation activity! As we hear often, "You can't teach that!" You can't teach children to just, "Be excited!" "Give it

all you've got!" "Give 100 percent!" "Gut it out!" They learn these things in the heat of the battle. Could it be that Paul's "bodily exercise profits a little" might just be what we are talking about here? Paul also referred to athletic participation when he said that those who run in a race (1 Corinthians 9) "run to win." Your children need outlets to *run*! They need to see in their own way through their activities what it takes to run and to win *and* to lose. Some of the greatest life lessons ever learned have been through losing. As parents, we need to be right there in that arena with both the wins and the losses.

The second part of Colossians 3:23 is that part of the verse that reads, "And not for men." It is right here that things begin to fall apart regarding parenting. Both the child and the parent can easily get swept away into the storms of "and not for men." By this, I am speaking of the phenomenon that occurs when our participation turns to *the game and the acclaim*! We, parents, begin thinking of what this could mean for all of us when, "My child is the best," when, "My child is playing on the best team," when, "My child may play in college. My child may be the next MLB, NFL, NBA star, and beyond." On the other side of this is the child athlete (star). Let me take you beyond this thinking to a scenario that appears later after athletics and music and art and drama are of the past. I have been meeting professionally with many married couples who have come for marital help to try and piece things back together. I have had many (not just one or two) of the men in these marriages who were good athletes in high school and some in college. I began to see a striking resemblance that these former athletes had with one another. Their athletic careers eventually ended. Some hung up the cleats after high school; some played on into their college years. As a good high school athlete, each one attested to the approval, the awards, the newspaper articles, the attention, and much more. But as I said, it all came to an end. *Then what?* The reason they were in my office for marital counseling was that they had been unfaithful to their wives and family through infidelity and affairs or pornography. One conclusion I drew was that they had been surviving essentially on all the *acclaim from men* for years, and when that pot ran dry, they too ran dry. They had an emotional tank full of awards, news articles, approval, and attention; and when they were no longer the "item," they suffered from a dangerous mental state of *unmet emotional needs.* They sought out fulfillment and a "high" in people and places that their wives and children could not fill. Need

I say that this all probably started way back in some of the early years of athletic participation? Parents, please keep some composure in all of your children's extracurricular activities, and help them to play, learn, participate, excel, lose, give it all they've got, and have fun.

5. Be *mentors for life*. As is so aptly stated often, *it takes a village to raise a child*. Honestly, parents, we need all the help we can get. There have been so many coaches, mentors, teachers, interested church family, and neighbors who have been part of our children's lives. Were it not for them, there are many life lessons our children would have never learned. Is it not true that in any school, the most popular on any staff are the coaches and extracurricular group leaders? Who is the most popular person in the church for your child? Undoubtedly, it was either the youth minister or Sunday school teacher. Parents, do your work of laying the foundation. Check out the "lay of the land" of available key people for your child to engage with and encourage or, as stated earlier, "train up a child in the way he should go."

You may remember Hannah, the wife of Elkanah and the mother of Samuel. Hannah had prayed fervently for a child and that if the Lord blessed her with this child, she would give him to the Lord. She did just that! At about the age of three, the parents followed through with their promise to give Samuel to the Lord. They left him at the temple with Eli. I am certainly not asking you to give your child away as Hannah did; however, as parents, we can play a major role in making sure that our children have influential and spiritually motivated mentors as they grow and mature. It may be a youth minister or other minister, it may be a coach or teacher, it could be an uncle or aunt, or it may be a neighbor or friend. The point here is that our children need mentors and role models outside of their parents who reinforce the principles and values that we hold true in our homes.

Their Very Own Words

In the preceding section, we have been discussing what I called the Significant Seven. I consider these to be the heart of this research. In them are found the most significant indicators that led to the success these families experienced with their children. The Significant Seven are the principles that were generally practiced by *all* or *practically all* couples in this research. As I pulled this information together, it made all the sense in the world to look at their top responses—hence, the Significant Seven.

We turn now to a series of questions that were posed to them. These are questions that cover a variety of parenting issues and concerns. The Significant Seven was *my* synthesis of what I saw. These are *their* words. I thought it fitting to include these here:

1. No parent is always going to be on the same exact page. There are always going to be areas

in which you may disagree. How did you handle this in your parenting approach?

   a) "We discussed our differences in private, and once we made a decision, we stuck to it."

   b) "We usually held off discussing our differences until the kids were not around."

   c) "We did not differ much, but when we did, it was not in front of the children."

   d) "It is very rare that we disagree. They have seen us disagree, but we never have big arguments."

   e) "We did not hide our differences, but we did not let things get out of control."

2. How did the parenting you received growing up affect the way you parent your children?

   a) "100% affected our parenting. The things we experienced, we brought into our parenting approach."

   b) "No, we learned as we went through the different parenting phases."

   c) "Probably not. We were fortunate to have kids that gave us no reason to be parented the way we were."

   d) "Not in all aspects. Spiritually, yes. Sports and other areas, not so much."

   e) "Yes, in discipline and in valuing our love for each other."

3. Describe the "village" it took to raise your kids.

   a) "Grandparents and church family."

b) "Extended family that held the same spiritual values. Also church, family, and grandparents."

c) "Grandparents, school, family, and church."

d) "Surrogate grandparents and church family."

e) "Church, Christian school family, and very active grandparents, aunts, uncles, and cousins."

4. What are some of the traditions and family rituals that your family practiced?

a) "We ate dinner at the table every night. We had Friday night movie night with dinner in front of the TV. We always had Sunday dinner with family members at one of their houses."

b) "Camping, family dinners, and movie night."

c) "We ate together as a family, had evening devotions, sang songs when we traveled, and we visited the same favorite spots for vacation."

d) "We shared scriptures and observed holidays in special ways, especially Christmas and Christmas Eve. We would dress in special attire and always read *The Night Before Christmas*. We would take trips to the mountains in the fall and the beach in the summer. We would visit entertainment sites. We had dogs. We shared politics. We loved college football as well as certain movies and TV shows."

e) "We would take yearly vacations. Holidays, especially Thanksgiving and Christmas, were very special. We would go to our grandparents' houses. We would go looking at lights at Christmas. We always held hands whenever we prayed at home or church. I [Mom] would read Bible stories, and Dad would always lie down with the kids to get them to sleep."

f) "Holidays with parties, birthdays, yearly vacations, boy's nights, Saturday morning breakfasts out, Friday night movies, and ordering food out."

g) "Christmas mornings, Dad would pass out gifts one at a time. We all would say, "I love you," before leaving or hanging up the phone."

5. As you think back on your parenting experience, what do you wish you could have done differently?

a) "Less emphasis on sports and more living for the Lord."

b) "More fun time on days off rather than cleaning, and more family devotionals."

c) "Relax more and enjoy with the children."

d) "I [Dad] could have been more understanding."

e) "We may have been a little too strict."

6. Was there a feeling of mutual openness in the family?

a) "There was openness and honesty, whether the topic was good or bad. Our kids were loved unconditionally."

b) "Each child was unique. We focused on each child's uniqueness with support and encouragement. We gave both positive and negative criticism, and no disrespect was tolerated."

c) "We tried to get them to see every situation from another's point of view, not theirs."

d) "We were strict but loving. We expected them to live by our family rules, and if they didn't, there were always consequences. In all this, there was love."

e) "We balanced criticism and objectivity. We could be positively critical. We [parents] were balanced in our personalities."

f) "We allowed our children to try new things and to face the consequences. We would support them, no matter the outcome."

g) "We always had conversations on how things could have been done better so there could be a better game plan next time."

    h) "We taught them right from wrong, and they knew right from wrong. We were fortunate they were true to their values."

7. Was pornography or the existence of strong sexual literature or videos in your home a parenting problem for you?

    a) "We had none of this in our home."

    b) "We looked at their phones and closely monitored them regularly."

    c) "Not a problem."

    d) "Did not have to deal with this."

    e) "Did not have to deal with these things."

    f) "We had one computer in our house, and it was kept in our room. Our kids never had one until they went off to college. Our kids were the last ones in their class to get cell phones."

    g) "None in their rooms. No phones. Very little social media…"

    h) "I regret not limiting video games. We bought the kids cell phones when they began driving."

8. As parents, how did you handle that inevitable "the birds and the bees" discussion?

    a) "They already knew."

    b) "Dad planned a day out with each boy, and then he gave them a BB gun."

c) "They were more embarrassed than we were. We just tried to be truthful and honest."

d) "We just deferred to God's instructions."

e) Boy and girl: "He didn't talk much. She did. We were very forthright. If the world is going to be direct, then we had to be just as direct, coming from the opposite side. We referred to Bible teachings on premarital sex. We used real-life examples of those who made bad decisions. We even used examples of some of their peers."

f) "We never had the 'the birds and the bees' talk. We just taught the Bible approach to sex. We bought a book and gave it to them to read. They all joke about this book now."

g) "We never talked about it. We just taught them that sex was to be held until marriage."

h) "He [Dad] would talk to the boys. She [Mom] would talk to the girls. We would talk about it very matter-of-factly from God's plan."

i) "We covered it naturally as it came up, filling in any details as they became age-appropriate."

j) "Mom discussed sex with the children."

9. Were there some things that were considered taboo subjects that just never really came out at home?

   a) "They realized we were not perfect, that we loved them, and that we loved each other."

   b) "We always welcomed discussion at the dinner table; while praying at night; riding in the car; at family meetings; and when we would discuss family plans, schedules, or other necessary topics. We invited their opinions. They knew they were loved because they heard it every day."

   c) "We always validated them and guided them without judgment."

   d) "We always talked about everything. We let them know they were loved, no matter what, and encouraged them to come to us about different topics. We talked of choices and consequences and that even if forgiven, there were still consequences."

   e) "We were kind of *old school*. We felt like there were some things that parents and children don't discuss. It came down to being a parent versus being a friend. In this, we never instilled shame or guilt. We never *dumped* on them."

   f) "They knew they could talk to us about anything. We would not embarrass or judge them. We would not betray them or their confidence in us as parents yet, at the same time, would not condone them in their ideas or feelings not according to God's teaching. They would share every day everything that was said or done during the day. It was hard on us when we knew certain things but could not act on them."

g) "Nothing was off-limits, and we loved them, no matter what."

h) "We always told them they could talk to us about anything. One would keep things to himself. The other is embarrassed to talk about anything."

10. Did your children experience seeing you, as a couple, display physical affection toward one another? Has this affected their choice of a mate?

a) "Yes, they see the love we have for each other, and they want the same for themselves."

b) "Yes, they chose spouses with our same values. We prayed about this from the beginning of our first pregnancy. We love our sons and daughters-in-law."

c) "Our daughter used to say that she wanted to marry a man like her daddy. Each male child married a woman with dispositions like their mom. They love their children and want them to live godly lives."

d) "Yes, they have close relationships with both of us and feel safe and comfortable."

e) "They all married Christians with strong moral standards.

11. How did you deal with anger in your family setting?

a) "We treated each other with respect and honor. We used time-outs and had them write down why they were angry and what they expected. We emphasized them asking for forgiveness and giving forgiveness."

b) "Disengage until the angry person calmed and have them go into a room alone."

c) "Let them express their feelings, but said, "*Be angry, and sin not.*" We tried to get them to calm down before dealing with the issue."

d) "We pledged before marriage to practice the Bible principle of not letting the sun go down on wrath. This lasted about five years until one time, I got mad about something and didn't talk to my spouse for two days, so we discussed the situation and came to an agreement civilly. We don't always agree, so it takes both of us. If we end up hurting one another, we go back to the original "don't let the sun go down on your wrath." We apologize and ask for forgiveness before sleep."

e) "No one had anger problems in our family. She [Mom] tends to be a little impatient. We just deal with it."

f) "He [Dad] had the issue. She [Mom] helped us all work through it."

g) "Any time anger led to disrespect, consequences followed."

h) "We always tried to reason it out."

12. *How did you deal with dishonesty or lying in the family?*

a) "Our kids lived in a high consequential environment; high expectations. We were hard on our own kids (despite what others thought of us); not just our standards, but God's standards."

b) "We believe our kids were basically honest; they may have stretched the truth in some cases, but we do not believe lying was one of their flaws."

c) "We always stressed honesty and the consequences for lying were more severe."

d) "This was not a major issue; it did occur some. We discussed it and prayed."

e) "I can't say it never happened. We were big on telling the truth; they did not want to be caught in a lie; they knew there would be heavy consequences."

13. How would you describe discipline in your family?

   a) "There were always consequences. We constantly pointed it out, brought it to their attention, and related it to biblical teaching."

   b) "Consistency and follow-through and consequences that *fit the crime*. We would try to get them to see how what they affected others."

   c) "We set rules and explained the consequences, but we did not have a lot of rules. We showed biblical examples of the consequences of behavior."

   d) "By the time our kids were of the age of understanding, they knew our expectations of them, which was treating people with respect, not using bad language or speaking derogatorily of anyone, respecting their teachers, studying hard and getting a college education, being in the church and taking part, treating young ladies with respect for boys, and acting respectfully for girls. They were not perfect. They made mistakes, but they knew we were there for them when they failed."

   e) "We definitely had consequences and expectations. We were hard on them because they were held to a higher standard."

f) "We tried to be consistent. Children need to be responsible for their actions. Actions have consequences."

g) "We allowed them to endure the consequences of their actions, no matter how badly we wanted to alleviate their hurt."

h) "They were taught to obey their parents and grandparents from the time they were small children. They were taught to respect adults. They received discipline when they disobeyed family rules."

i) "We tried to be consistent with our discipline. We didn't just threaten. We followed through with discipline."

Summary

In thinking about how to bring this book to a close, I have no better way than to use some very special thoughts expressed by three of the parents involved in this study. These responses were not answers to questions, nor were they prompted in any way. These are statements made "along the way" during their experience of participating in this project. What they say is so fitting, and it brings together everything I had hoped to share as a summary. There is another parent who made some very meaningful comments that I included earlier (see application 2 of the Significant Seven) that could also easily be included in this summary.

1. "Our whole life, we tried to base upon living for Christ. That underlying precept set the rules for our jobs, our discipline, our decisions, our friends, our habits, our traditions, and our entertainment. The kids knew that just because their friends did something or were allowed to go somewhere, it was *never* an appropriate rea-

son for them to do something. They learned very early that we were not responsible for their friends, but God made us responsible for our own kids. We always encouraged the boys at a very early age to lead prayers, read scriptures, and attend Bible programs. We went with all the kids on mission trips and were counselors at Bible camps with them. We did service projects together as a family for neighbors and needy church members. We felt that the greatest way to teach was by example. We laughed a lot and had fun, and still do. We always supported and encouraged each other in our spiritual lives and spiritual growth, and we still do."

2. "We feel our children are upright, godly, moral individuals who are raising upright, godly, moral children themselves. We made a lot of mistakes and maybe did a few things right. We used to say that they made it to adulthood *by the grace of God*. When you get as old as we are and look back, you recognize a few really important things. Here are a few: First, we have heard it said, "The best gift a father can give his children is to love and respect their mother. The best gift a mother can give her children is to love and respect their father!" We believe this to be ever true. Second, the book of James speaks of the *unbridled tongue*. We feel that more family relationships have been severed by

parents saying harsh and hurtful things to their children—berating them, shaming them, and guilting them—especially when children are grown, have chosen their mates, and are raising their own children. Parents should be especially careful in choosing their words. Encourage. Don't criticize. Third, our daughter has the following hanging in her den:

In our house…

> We do second chances.
> We do grace.
> We do, "I love you."
> We do, "I'm sorry."
> We do laughter.
> We do family.

We pray that she learned a little of that from us!"

3. We feel like raising our boys was easy compared to a lot of other parents. We felt like they were blessings to us. Their dad was very good at teaching the boys how to be responsible with their money. They both started working when they were young, and we made them save some and then give some at church. Their dad always wanted to be close to them since his father was never close to him. Our family has always

joked with one another, especially their dad and them. We wanted them to enjoy spending time with us."

Personal Remarks

If I might take a scripture out of its context, please indulge me. In the book of 3 John 4, John says, "It always gives me the greatest joy when I hear that my children are walking in the truth." I know that John was speaking of his children in the faith; however, there is no harm done to this text to apply his principle to parents and children. I am sure John would agree with me when I say this, and most likely, he would feel the same way because I know that to the believers, there is truly no greater joy than to know that their children are walking in faith and not only walking themselves but also that they are leading their own children in that same walk. The parents in this study could all say (and I mean every single one of them) that they have an unquenchable joy and happiness that their children are walking in the truth. I am so happy and blessed that they chose to participate and that they have willingly shared their lives with all of us.

This task has been a physically, mentally, and emotionally daunting one. It has taken about four years and untold hours to pull it all together. Had it not been for the COVID-19 pandemic, I would probably have been working another year or more (quarantine has its advantages). I have spent many sessions with God, praying and pleading for his insights and for his Spirit to continue to push and nudge me in the finishing of this project. I do not regret one minute of all this.

If there was to be a regret, it would be all the time that took me away from those I love, and I am speaking first and foremost of my wife, Amy. She has been such an encouragement in this work. She is a true *partner* in every sense of the word. Without such an influence in my life, most likely, this project might never have come to fruition.

Ultimate appreciation goes out to these couples who took the time to share their parenting lives with us and to bless all of us in the same ways that they have been a blessing to their own children. I used the following analogy in many of the parenting classes I taught: Think about your parenting experience. It can sometimes feel like a very lonely and uphill battle that goes on under the roof of your house, and that is the extent of it. The truth is the opposite is really the case. Your family becomes ground zero for generations to come. Just think of the influence, either positive or negative, that each member of your family has and will have. Each spouse and child will have their own sphere of influence as they move out into the world. Other individuals, neighborhoods, places of work and business, schools, churches, and the entire world are affected either positively or negatively by what transpires under the roofs of your houses. This changes the perspective, doesn't it? These couples brought thirty children into this world. Think with me for just a moment. Do you suppose those thirty kids will ever have friends? Of course (just think how many Facebook friends most kids have). Will they ever be a member of any classroom, club, or team? Will they ever have jobs? Will they ever have a best friend or a close group of friends? Will they ever be employed and have work friends? This logic could go on and on, but I think you know where I am going with this. Just to throw out an arbitrary number, and I can safely say that each of these thirty children who have grown up in the families we have had the privilege of getting to know might easily and directly affect the lives of at least two hundred other people (and this is a very conservative number). So thirty lives and souls have turned into six thousand lives and souls just at the stroke of a pen. I am just trying to turn our attention to the gravity of the responsibility we have as parents. So my thanks goes out to all the couples in this project for the amazing part you have played in making this world a much better place.

Finally, God, thank you for all you do in this world to help us as parents. Without your grace, mercy, and love, we would not make it. Without your Word, we would not have the blueprint for parenting success. Without your Holy Spirit, we would not have the day-to-day pushing, prodding, and nudging we need when the parenting task seems undoable.

Recommendations

Only love invests the time and energy to tackle such a daunting task and worthy project of thorough research, identifying the practical realities needed to be lived out in individuals and families that naturally translate into living well, both now and for the next generations. I encourage you to take this compilation of life 'stories' and nuggets of 'practical wisdom' as a slow read, almost like a devotional, allowing its encouragement and wisdom to seep into the fabric of your life choices to positively impact your family's life and children's future.

Perry Sanderford, PhD, LPC
Chief administrator of Crossroads
Christian Marriage and Family
Counseling of Mississippi
(Jackson, Pearl, Ridgeland, Laurel,
Hattisburg, and Clinton)

Navigating parenting is difficult enough when doing it by yourself. I highly recommend *Parenting from Down in the Trenches* as a must-read for all parents. Benny takes a practical Christian approach to the challenges of parenting. The effective tools he provides are full of wisdom, experience, and insight. This will be a book I will continue to recommend to families.

Jennifer Kughn
Children's minister at Gateway
Church of Christ (Pensacola, Florida)

"The book I wrote, Race Against Time, tells the inside story of a historic race for justice. Families, communities, and others benefited from this justice. Parenting From Down In The Trenches, too, seeks to bring relief to families and communities by restoring strength to the family unit through the practice of parenting principles that God has taught us. Benny Hunton has long provided wise guidance to struggling parents. He backs that up with experience by interviewing three generations of successful parents. Read this book to learn how you too can succeed in your parenting efforts.

Jerry Mitchell is the author of Race Against Time, a best seller about his efforts to bring justice to klansmen decades after they got away with murder. Mitchell is the winner of more than 30 national awards. He left the Clarion Ledger in Jackson, Mississippi after 30 years of working as an investigative reporter and founded the Mississippi Center for Investigative Reporting, a nonprofit.

About the Author

Richard Hunton, affectionately known as Benny, is a licensed mental health counselor in northwest Florida. He is presently licensed as an LPC (licensed professional counselor) in the state of Mississippi and an LMHC (licensed mental health counselor) in the state of Florida. He has been a licensed counselor for twenty-five years. Benny has been working with the children, youth, and families for forty-nine years as a coach, classroom teacher, guidance director, youth minister, and minister. He and his wife, Amy, teach marriage enrichment workshops, parenting workshops, and grandparenting workshops. He has served as a court-appointed parenting instructor for many years in the state of Florida. He holds a bachelor's degree in Bible and religious education from Faulkner University in Montgomery, Alabama, and a bachelor's degree in health, PE, and recreation from Lipscomb University in Nashville, Tennessee. He also holds a master's degree in counseling from the University of Central Florida in Orlando, Florida.

His credentials go much deeper than degrees and employment. The passions that drive him are first, his Lord; second, his family and youth; and third, his love for sports. He knew early on that sports would be a great way to reach the hearts of kids, thus helping them to find the Lord of their life also. Thus, he pursued his higher education in the fields of religious education, physical education, and counseling. He feels that God has blessed him beyond measure to be able to work in Christian education and to use coaching as a means of reaching youth.

Benny and Amy now reside in Pensacola, Florida. They manage a counseling ministry serving various churches, dealing with individual, family, marital, and adolescent issues.